DIRTY LITTLE SECRETS

ERICA ORLOFF
AND JoAnn BAKER

Dirty Little
SECRETS

*True Tales and Twisted
Trivia About Sex*

St. Martin's Griffin
New York

www.stmartins.com

BOOK DESIGN BY CASEY HAMPTON

Library of Congress Cataloging-in-Publication Data

Orloff, Erica.
    Dirty little secrets : true tales and twisted trivia about sex / Orloff/Baker.
        p. cm.
    Includes bibliographical references and index.
    ISBN 0-312-26949-8
    1. Sex—Folklore.   2. Sex—Anecdotes.   I. Baker, Joann.   II. Title.

GR462.O74 2001
306.7—dc21   00-045853

First Edition: February 2001

10 9 8 7 6 5 4 3 2 1

To Muffy and Dick,
a perfectly matched pair

CONTENTS

ACKNOWLEDGMENTS

Orloff and Baker would like to thank Kathy and Marc Levinson for originally believing in this project; Jay Poynor for his support, encouragement, and sense of humor; and Pam Morrell for her help and support. They also thank Charles Spicer and Joe Cleemann for all their expertise.

Orloff, as always, would like to thank her family: Walter, Maryanne, Stacey, Jessica, and of course, Alexa, Nick, and Bella. She would like to thank John Diaz for his unending belief in her.

Baker would like to thank certain staff members of the M F Library; Elizabeth Parsons (you hilarious woman, you); Fred Youngs, Mike DeGaspris, Rick Brown, and Chris Brown for their collective thoughts on getting the point across without saying it; and last, but never least, Bob, Joe, and Chris.

DIRTY LITTLE SECRETS

1

ONCE UPON A TIME

Once upon a time, sex was a simple affair—but we're talking a really long time ago. So, we might as well start with the pri-

mordial ooze, when life consisted of single-cell organisms. These microscopic forms were so basic they didn't even have genders. To reproduce, they just split in two. But whenever the population outgrew its environment and sustaining life was more difficult, some of the organisms fused together instead. To improve their chances of survival, the cells chose fusion partners as different from themselves as possible (probably causing their friends and relatives to wonder why two such opposites would be attracted to one another).

Eventually, more and more cells glommed together (no one said this book is scientific), and life forms got bigger and more complex until finally there were stable species with two distinct genders.

From this lowly beginning, males and females have been relentlessly pursuing each other. But it wasn't until modern man arrived on the scene that sex became a complicated matter involving spiritual, social, and political ramifications.

THOU SHALT BETTER STOP BOFFING

The ancient Greeks and Romans have a reputation for enjoying licentious behavior, while it seems as if the ancient Jews were always getting smote down for it. Since both cultures understood that people have strong sex drives, how is it they developed such diverse attitudes? Probably because humans have one instinct even stronger than the one to procreate—the one to survive. According to some theorists, because both the Greeks and Romans lived in relatively small areas, as their civilizations grew so did the need for population control. Since sex and procreation went hand in hand, and the invention of the pill was a few millennia away, alternative methods of sexual satisfaction were not only accepted, but to some degree, encouraged. Some men kept sterile mistresses, others took male lovers. Homosexual activity was regarded as natural enough to be woven into the legends of their gods and heroes. The parameters of acceptability, however, are a little ironic. While sodomy between an adult male mentor and his adolescent student was expected, a monogamous homosexual relationship between two grown men was a social no-no. Go figure. And sex with a child not yet through puberty was illegal.

At one point, the Greeks also controlled their population by exiling fertile, unmarried women to the Isle of Lesbos. Since the only sex to be had there was with other women, it's no wonder Lesbians became synonymous with female homosexuals.

The ancient Jewish civilization had a completely different problem. They lived in a fruitful land surrounded by hostile neighbors with much larger populations. For the Jews, increasing their numbers was as necessary to survival as controlling the populace was to the Greeks and Romans. So the ultimate goal of sex was conception, which eventually translated to conception being the only respectable goal for sex.

By the time Moses came trotting down the mountain with his rules on rock, communal morality frowned upon alternative sexual practices. Masturbation, homosexuality, bestiality, and prostitution all got negative press in the Old Testament. (And coveting your neighbor's wife isn't allowed, although knocking up your brother's widow is not only okay, it's a duty.) But marital sex was regarded with approval and is celebrated in the Song of Songs.

Considering the Good Book's rather stringent regulations regarding sexual relations, it's rather odd that a common euphemism for intercourse with a woman is "to know her in the biblical sense."

Since the first Christians had been Jewish, the newly created religion held to Jewish beliefs regarding sex. But by 500 A.D., even intercourse for procreation was viewed as a necessary evil. Celibacy was a holy trait. This was partly because of the teachings of St. Augustine. He had been quite a wild one, taking both male and female lovers, until he renounced his evil ways. Once he tucked the old one-eyed snake away for good, he wrote about his experiences and his interpretation of them.

FEET IN THE STIRRUPS, KNEES APART

Gyne, the root word for gynecology comes from the Greek and means bearer of children. Gynecologists, however, do not bear children for a living. They are more like inspectors of child-bearing equipment. They do their job using a miner's hat and ice-cold instruments.

Lust, he felt, was the defining difference between Man and God. He believed Adam and Eve were cast from the Garden of Eden for their sin of sexual lust and that, as a result, all humans were burdened from birth with this original sin.

Meanwhile, on the other side of the world, the Chinese, Hindu, and Islamic people had an entirely different perspective on sex. A celebrated facet of life, sexual activity was neither restricted nor regarded as negative. The *Kama Sutra* (a manual on sexual variety and positions) was first compiled around the time Augustine was promoting a chaste life.

A LITTLE ICE IN THE CODPIECE AND VOILA!

Christianity quickly spread, and the number of followers grew with each generation. By the Middle Ages, the church was so powerful in Europe that it eclipsed secular society, and religious rules were synonymous with common law. Church leaders dictated sexual repression for the multitude, but certain members of the upper class could have "courtly love." A highly suspect custom, courtly love sprung from the idea that while marriages (which were usually arranged) generally resulted in love, that love was somewhat sullied by the obligatory nasty stuff that went on between the sheets. In contrast, courtly lovers were thought to have a pure love, untainted by sex, for one another. To prove their love was the courtly variety, the pair was tested by being stripped naked and made to lie down next to each other for a period of time. If no signs of lust passed between them, they were free to spend time together without a chaperone. (The idea that Lord Muffwilling and Lady Peterlove wouldn't eventually consummate their relationship once out of the public eye is certainly a curiously naive supposition. Perhaps because the priesthood attracted a fair amount of homosexuals who were capable of loving a woman without lusting for her, they based their assumptions on their own experience.) Apparently, commoners were incapable of "pure" love, since this practice was only acceptable among the elite.

BUT HONESTLY, M'LORD, THIS BELT DOESN'T GO WITH MY ENSEMBLE!

It was also during the Middle Ages that technology reared its sometimes ugly head in the form of a new invention—the chastity belt. The belt allowed men to lock up their wives and daughters, who were considered property. Entirely made of metal, the chastity belt sat on a woman's hips and a molded band, attached to the front, went between the legs and locked onto the back of the belt. Two small holes in the band provided an outlet for elimination but were too small for any kind of penetration. Whether a chastity belt was made of ornately carved gold or crudely molded iron, it was heavy, rigid, and it restricted movement. But these were the least of the wearer's

LORDY, LORDY, GIVE THE GIRL SOME CREDIT

Clear up until the mid-1600s, it was generally believed that teeny tiny humans resided within the viscous ejaculation of men. These mini-folks just needed a nice warm womb so they could grow up to be babies. This theory meant that as long as a man could ejaculate, he was capable of producing offspring. So, invariably it was a woman's fault if a couple failed to have children.

Anatomy professor Dr. Gabriel Fallopius noted the existence of both the ovaries and tubes (yup, those fallopian things) in women sometime in the mid-1500s, but another 100 years would go by before anyone figured out that those extra parts had a purpose. The discovery came, not from a scientist or physician, but from a haberdasher.

Antoine van Leewenhoek ground glass into lenses as a hobby and succeeded in creating a microscope with a high enough resolution to see cells. The world's first microbiologist, this Dutch haberdasher made numerous discoveries, one of which is that women produce and contribute an egg to the procreation process.

problems. A woman could be locked into a belt for extended periods of time while her husband was away. Even with very frequent bathing, hygiene was extremely difficult. Menstrual flow and bowel movements could easily cause bacterial infections that could turn deadly. The metal bands could chafe to bleeding, and the resulting sores were also an open invitation to bacteria. If a woman lost weight, it might be easier for her to keep herself clean, but the chafing would increase. If she gained weight, the opposite was true. And if she gained enough weight, she could lose circulation below the belt. One of the original intentions of putting a woman in a chastity belt was to prevent rape. But it seems logical that a rapist (who is more likely to commit the crime out of aggression, not desire) would be more likely to kill his victim if he found the goodies inaccessible.

Both the Protestant Reformation and resurgence of the arts and humanism of the sixteenth and seventeenth centuries brought a more relaxed attitude toward sex. Not to say slutting around was encouraged, but things did loosen up somewhat, and the customs of courtly love and chastity belts faded into the past.

A BRAND-NEW WORLD, BUT THE SAME OLD IDEAS

Mainstream Europe might have been less uptight about sex in the 1700s, but in America the Puritan ethic in New England was alive and well. Laws against perversion (pretty much any sex act that wasn't intercourse between married couples) abounded and proscribed punishments ranged from public humiliation (as in Nathaniel Hawthorn's *The Scarlet Letter*) to the death penalty, with everything from whippings, to stockade or jail time in between. To prevent impropriety, rules for single men and women were very specific and addressed a multitude of situations, including when (only during daylight, unless engaged) and how (man on the street side, never touching more than a woman's elbow) a pair could walk together in public.

Americans who had less interest in purity could pack up and head for the Wild West, where prostitution abounded. Lawmen

PLEASE, DON'T TELL ME YOU'RE ONLY NINE

In view of the Victorian attitude toward sexual behavior, certain laws during the era seem particularly incongruous. In 25 states, the legal age of consent was only 10, making children victims of both prostitution and sale for marriage. A public outcry in 1886 eventually caused all but five states to raise the age of consent, but many of them only brought it to 13 or 14.

were too few and too busy to bother with blow jobs for hire. And because the number of men so far exceeded that of women, prostitutes were a welcome diversion.

I THOUGHT I TOLD YOU, THIS BELT DOESN'T GO WITH MY ENSEMBLE!

In yet another cycle, Europeans were going puritanical again, and by the Victorian Era of the 1800s, "proper" behavior was so sexually repressed that offering a lady a breast or thigh of chicken was considered offensive. In fact, offering a leg was also rude. Women's clothing was so modest that heaven forbid a neck or ankle was seen. In many homes, piano legs became victims of virtue and were kept covered with skirts. (Perhaps they believed Fido wasn't the only one that might find himself in amorous pursuit of furniture legs.) Prudishness also reigned in home libraries, where books written by male authors were not shelved next to those written by females (except for authors married to one another).

THERE'S NO ONE BUT EWE

Horny farm guys have occasionally looked to the back end of their animals for relief, but in Massachusetts during the 1600s the practice of buggery (a euphemism for sex with animals) could have devastating results. Whether the guilty party was a grown man or a young boy, those caught bonking livestock were quickly put to death. First, however, the offender was usually required to watch while the animal was killed. Doing away with the victim came from the belief that sex between humans and animals could produce offspring. The concept of a half-human species was terrifyingly real to these early Americans, and they felt it was imperative to prevent such births.

The chastity belt reappeared during this time, but with a few differences. For one thing, some women chose to wear a chastity belt for protection. In those cases, the woman herself had the key, and she used the belt only outside the home. For women locked into them, cleanliness was quite a bit easier with a bidet. And some girls were put into chastity belts by their parents to prevent masturbation.

WE WANT TO BE PRUDES, TOO!

Upper-class Americans were quick to hop on the Victorian bandwagon of repression, and they brought it into the political arena. Groups such as "The American Society for the Prevention of Licentiousness and Vice and the Promotion of Morality" and "The American Society for Promoting Observance of the Seventh Commandment" were gaining a voice. These gangs of moral conservatism wanted to stop prostitution and save "fallen women" from an eternity in hell. These groups weren't very successful at eliminating brothels, but they enjoyed some political clout and sowed the early seeds of the temperance movement. But, as with every mainstream movement, there are those who have a different set of values and rebel against the status quo. So while culturally correct households covered their furniture legs to keep from offending delicate sensibilities, pornography flourished underground. Officials passed laws regarding censorship and banning porno, but the law had little effect on the popularity of erotic material. At the start of the Civil War, officers prosecuted soldiers caught with lewd material but quickly determined their efforts were futile. So, within the military the censorship laws were pretty much ignored.

In fact, many sexual beliefs and practices of the time were not consistent with one another. While Victorian followers were pretending s*x didn't really exist, some doctors began recommending ways husbands could bring their wives to orgasm.

IF WE CAN'T MAKE IT GO AWAY, LET'S HIDE IT IN A MENTAL INSTITUTION

Throughout the first three-quarters of the nineteenth century, homosexuality was not acceptable, but "romantic love" between friends was. A Victorian etiquette book for women suggests that the practice of girls touching, stroking, and kissing each other was a private affair and should never be done in front of a gentleman. Likewise, it wasn't considered odd for a man to write a letter confessing his love to his male friend. Yet, despite the homoerotic nature of these relationships, sex acts like cunnilingus or fellatio between couples of the same gender was scandalous. The custom of romantic love and society's tolerance for it might have come, in part, from the constant separation of the sexes. This is especially true of students at boarding schools, soldiers fighting the Civil War, and the cowboys working in the Old West. For many, indulging in homosexual relationships was born, not of preference, but of long periods of time spent in single-gender situations. For those people who did prefer their own sex, however, the cowboy life reputedly drew a number of men specifically because of the freedom to pursue an alternative lifestyle. And there are accounts of lesbians who dressed and lived as men so they could earn men's wages and openly engage in relationships with other women.

Morality groups got vocal in their opposition to homosexuality, and in the 1880s the American Medical Society labeled homosexuality as a perverse mental disease. Within a year, laws forbidding "acts against nature" (a euphemism for sodomy) appeared on the books in most states. Gays caught in the act could avoid prosecution by pleading insanity.

ALL THAT JAZZ

Europeans, who started the whole Victorian thing, changed their tune and, by 1860, went so far as to legalize prostitution. While Americans never reached the same level of liberalism, the mainstream attitude started to relax by the turn of the century.

Life for middle- and upper-class Americans changed fast and furiously between 1900 and 1920. Males and females, previously separated most of the time, spent a majority of their days side by side. A growing economy allowed far more children to continue their education through the twelfth grade. High schools were jam-packed with hormonal teenagers who had much more time to socialize without the watchful eyes of their parents. Hollywood movies, a blossoming form of entertainment, promoted relationships based on mutual attraction rather than convenience or arrangement. Popular reading material included romance novels, true confession magazines, and Sigmund Freud's writings. These things all emphasized sexuality as an important force in the human experience—though each from a different perspective.

Women entered the workforce during World War I, which not only brought a mingling of genders on the job, but also in public, since necessity forced the women to go out unaccompanied. And once they started going out to work, women also started to go out for fun. Dance halls became extremely popular, and cars (still new but increasingly common) made nighttime entertainment easily accessible.

In the meantime, the government was persuaded by the temperance movement to make alcohol illegal. But Prohibition did nothing to stem the rise of sexuality which now simmered just below the surface. In the 1920s, hemlines were outrageously high and early jazz and rhythm and blues, with its sexual energy and explicit lyrics, was hot, hot, hot. Prohibition made underground bars all the more trendy, so you could find flappers dancing to the new music at many a local speakeasy.

Sexually speaking, a revolution for women was gathering

strength in the form of Margaret Sanger and her fight to bring birth control devices and education to American women (more about that later in this chapter).

The Roaring Twenties, the most decadent decade the country had seen, managed to bring sex far enough out of the darkness that, despite efforts to the contrary, the public hasn't since been persuaded back into Victorian prudery.

OH, THIS IS DEPRESSING

BAM . . . The stock market crash of 1929 brought serious economic hardship. During the Depression, many teens were forced to drop out of high school to work. Some had to work for free, replacing paid positions in the family business. Others scrambled to make whatever money they could, most of it going toward the family.

There were few people who could afford to go to dances, parties, or bars. Since these places of public amusement had been the main avenue for the wild abandon of the twenties, things tightened up sexually as well as financially. The somber mood of the period didn't help either, but some advances continued to be made. A man named Theodore Van de Velde wrote a book entitled *Ideal Marriage*. In it, he described methods of foreplay and a variety of positions for bonking in explicit detail. It was one of the first in a very long (and, as of yet, unending) line of "marriage" manuals that include the concept that relationships are better if the sex is enjoyed by both partners. The 1930s also marked the beginning of widespread acceptance that women . . . gasp . . . gasp had orgasms (probably prompting at least a few women to say, "well, duh!").

DON'TCHA JUST LOVE A MAN IN UNIFORM?

America's involvement in World War II drew unprecedented numbers of young women into the workforce and further out of the sphere of their parents' influence. Some of the women found soldiers just home from, or about to leave for, war extremely appealing and weren't particularly resistant to advances. Carrying on their own sort of "war effort," these women soon earned nicknames such as victory girls, khaki-wackies, and good-time Charlottes. Many married women got into the act, too. For the first time, they were holding down jobs and, with their husbands gone for extended periods of time, were enjoying an unfamiliar sense of independence. Historically more likely to be the victims of adultery, the war years provided wives the means, motive, and opportunity to instigate affairs themselves. Although the majority of women no doubt remained true to their absent husbands, enough engaged in extramarital gymnastics to subtly change the public perception of the female will and sex drive.

AW, MA. EVERYBODY DOES IT!

But the biggest change in Americans' perception of sexuality came in 1948 when zoologist Alfred Kinsey and two of his colleagues published *Sexual Behavior in the Human Male*. Known as the Kinsey Report, the book was based on over 12,000 personal interviews, and the findings were shocking. Most mainstream critics blasted the book, calling it immoral and anti-family, but the public found the information fascinating. Kinsey presented his results dispassionately, in scientific terms, and

FIVE COMMON CLAIMS ABOUT MASTURBATION

It will make you go blind.
It will cause hair to grow on your palms.
It will make you sterile.
Your dead grandmother will be watching.
It will cause insanity.

without judgment. The dry statistical data clearly indicated a chasm between rhetoric and actions, and most likely assuaged many a man's guilt. For instance, male masturbation was almost universal, despite its sinful reputation. In addition, 90 percent of the men had intercourse before marriage, and more than half the high school graduates who weren't married by the age of 25 had hired a prostitute. And more than one-third (37 percent to be exact) of the men interviewed said they had experienced at least one homosexual experience after puberty.

The Kinsey Report might have been a revelation, but that didn't mean the behaviors it charted were considered natural, or even personal business. The same year *Sexual Behavior in the Human Male* was published, all 48 states had sexual laws on their books, although they varied considerably. In Connecticut, a person caught committing adultery could get 5 years in prison whereas in New Mexico, adultery wasn't considered a crime. Fornication between two unmarried people was criminal in 33 states and could net someone a year in jail in Georgia. With the exception of only a few states, sodomy was a serious offense. In Nevada and Colorado, entering the backside or engaging in a blow job could result in a life sentence. Anal sodomy could get someone 1 to 10 years in California, but for

"oral perversion," one could receive 15 years. Georgia (apparently a state that preferred its citizens leave creativity outside
the bedroom door) recommended up to a life sentence for sodomy, but for bestiality the punishment was only 5 to 20 years.
Clearly, most of the sodomy laws were designed to allow the
arrest and conviction of gays.

ROCK 'N' ROLL, BOBBY SOX, AND BOYS WHO SHAKE THAT "THANG"

The strong double-standard of the 1950s left it to girls to set
sexual limits. Not that this was a particularly new idea, but once
again, the majority of teens were staying in school through high
school and many were going on to college. Most of them had
time and money to seek some kind of social life in their spare
time and that meant boys had more time to pressure girls to go
further faster, but a girl could be "ruined" by getting a reputation as a slut. It was tacitly accepted for college men to date
same-class women for social reasons, and working-class women
for sex. Those who were duped by men looking for nothing
more than a good time were usually left to deal with any re-
percussions on their own. The exception to this, for which
there was no public acknowledgment but was widely recognized as the norm, was engaged and/or seriously committed
couples. The expectation being, of course, that the sex was
monogamous and if a pregnancy resulted, the man would "do
right" and marry the woman.

But that was just the mainstream. A growing beatnik subculture was rebelling against the status quo and slowly having
an impact on the mass middle class. Artists, writers, and mu-

sicians were pushing the edge of the envelope with their work; and sex was, more often than not, the theme. Rock and roll, with its throbbing backbeat and sensual energy, was a favorite scapegoat for changing values, but philosophy, science, politics, media, and technology were all changing daily life so quickly that to have removed one of these in hopes of stemming the tide would have made little difference.

ALL YOU NEED IS LOVE

Disagreement over the Vietnam conflict threw America into a maelstrom of discontent, and the antiestablishment doctrine of the beatniks became the mantra of youth during the '60s. Baby boomers were coming of age, outnumbering their parents' generation, and rewriting the rules. Previously accepted prejudices and traditions were brought under fire, and issues ranging from the frivolous (such as hemlines and hair length) to the serious (such as civil rights and the draft) widened the gap between generations. Sexual behavior was, of course, challenged and changed. "Make love, not war" was a common refrain.

From "love-ins" to Woodstock, the sexual revolution of the 60s was highly visible. Newspaper, magazine, and television coverage of these events brought them into living rooms across the country. Late in the decade, capitalism (an anathema to the original antiestablishment movement) led entrepreneurs to open places like Plato's Retreat, which offered, for a price, a banquet of sexual activity including open orgies.

The women's movement was instrumental in the success of the sexual revolution. For them, the agenda was to throw off the bonds of constraint that permeated the climate of sex in the '50s. But while the '60s paved the way for women to finally say yes to recreational sex, for many it seemed to take away the right to say no.

LET'S SHAG, BABY

The free-spirited climate continued through the first half of the '70s, with all sorts of variations suddenly available. "Swingers," who participated in orgies, found each other through newspaper and magazine ads as well as places like Plato's Retreat, and some couples, even middle-class suburban ones, engaged in wife swapping (where married couples exchanged partners for the night). Sex shops were doing a booming business. They catered to those who wanted a little something other than another body. Whips, restraints, dildos, oils, and pornographic material were easily obtained and used to enhance sexual experiences.

Two major decisions also had an impact on the American view of sex. In 1973, the Supreme Court made its historic ruling on the *Roe v. Wade* case, legalizing abortion. And the following year the American Psychiatric Association removed homosexuality from its list of mental diseases.

By the late '70s, sex and procreation were irrevocably split. The variety of available birth control made intercourse without fear of pregnancy the norm. (Even the Catholic Church began regularly teaching its followers the rhythm method.) But the astounding split between boffing and babies came from the scientific development that allowed procreation without sex.

Tolerance for doing the wild thing wherever, whenever, and with whomever had a major impact on family life. The divorce rate soared, eventually reaching and remaining around 50 percent. But the shine really dulled on promiscuity in the late '70s when herpes suddenly emerged in near-epidemic proportions. A sexually transmitted and incurable disease, herpes profoundly affected many of the middle Americans who had been experimenting in the sexual arena. In addition, the number of teenage pregnancies increased dramatically, causing new concerns about liberal attitudes.

THE PENDULUM DOES ITS THING

Herpes might have put the initial damper on the sex train, but when the deadly AIDS virus appeared, the effect was even stronger. By 1984, the general public had retreated from unchecked promiscuity. Plus, the emergence of the political New Right with their pro-family, antiabortion conservatism brought new strength to former values. The federal judges appointed during the Reagan administration were sympathetic to the new wave of conservatism and in 1986, in a case entitled *Bowers v. Hardwick*, the Supreme Court ruled 5 to 4 that state sodomy laws were constitutional (undoubtedly a terrible *blow* to gays).

LOOK, NO HANDS!

As the extremes of the sexual revolution have faded, it seems as if the majority of Americans have become less obsessed with what consenting folks do behind closed doors. Once actually illegal, men and women cohabitating rarely even raises an eyebrow today. Discrimination based on sexual preference is

DOESN'T THIS BELT LOOK GREAT WITH MY ENSEMBLE?

For people who are into such things, chastity belts are available today through several manufacturers. They come in models for males as well as females and are made in a variety of materials. For those who just want to play, there are leather lock-ups, but for the truly serious, metal belts (from which it is impossible to escape) can also be purchased.

A perusal of Internet postings reveals that chastity belts appeal mainly to couples who are emotionally invested in control. Although sometimes tied (oops, no pun intended) to S & M practices, belts also provide pleasure to those who simply enjoy the concept of ownership.

Another attraction of chastity belts is the enforced chastity, so that the lockee (unable even to masturbate) has built up tremendous sexual tension by the time the keyholder sees fit to unlock his or her partner.

considered a violation of civil rights. And adultery has become fodder for talk shows as opposed to a matter for the courts.

The exception to this mind-your-own-business attitude is within the government. Members of the military have faced charges and been punished for affairs and, of course, Clinton was brought to the brink of disaster by investigations into the antics of the First Penis. This is particularly ironic since historically, many of the presidents who led the country during far more puritanical times had blatant affairs that everyone just sort of ignored. (More about this in Chapter 8.)

Sexual practices in the '90s include a number of hands-off interactions. Phone and cybersex, in which people stimulate one another through the use of words and imagination, have become popular methods of both avoiding diseases and venturing into fantasies without actually performing the acts. Mutual masturbation during these encounters allows each party to reach the big O. Debates over whether cybersex can be considered adultery, and whether these techno affairs are psychologically unhealthy, continue. Meanwhile, the computer persists as one of the myriad of ways humans titillate themselves.

DOING THE DEED WITHOUT PLANTING A SEED

Some say the defining difference between humans and all other species is the opposable thumb. Others say it is conscience. But this is a book about sex, so here is something else to think about. With the exception of humans, female animals only have intercourse when they are in season (or heat, or whatever you'd care to call the fertile times of their cycle). As for the human, however, well . . . girls just like to have fun. (Although those sociology types are likely to tell you this phenomenon has to do with the evolution from hunters and gatherers—that the cave woman was able to increase the chances her hunter man would return if he thought he'd get him some nookie upon returning to the home cave.)

Regardless, because of this difference, we humans are apt to be fornicating on any old day. Often, an orgasm, not a pregnancy, is the only goal of these intimate encounters. And so, from the beginning of recorded history, we have been devising methods of blocking, tackling, killing, and diverting determined sperms from their appointments with eggs.

Hope It Was Good . . .

In ancient China women swallowed mercury heated in oil as a form of birth control. A precursor to the "morning after" pill, this method actually worked because the mercury caused spontaneous abortions. Unfortunately, there was a minor side effect—mercury poisoning. Any woman who used this method repeatedly would go to an early grave.

Women in ancient Egypt also found something that was fairly effective. Although it wasn't deadly, it was seriously disgusting. Prior to intercourse, they inserted a mixture of honey and crocodile dung into their vaginas. The high acidity in the dung probably killed some of the sperm, and the mixture itself probably acted as a blockade. So, while it worked to some degree, it probably killed off any hope the woman might have had for receiving oral sex. (Polite guys probably claimed they were too pooped.)

Ancient Persians were smarter. They used sea sponges soaked in alcohol, iodine, quinine, or carbolic acid. The sponges acted as a barrier, and the liquids acted as a spermicide. Not only did these work better, they weren't fatal.

No Room at the Inn

During the Middle Ages, Arab herders put a stone into the uterus of female camels during long journeys. The stone, inserted by way of a hollow tube, prevented the camels from getting pregnant, which was important to the herders. A pregnant camel is very testy and will often lie down and refuse to budge.

The success of this early intrauterine device led to all sorts of objects being stuck into both human and animal uteruses. Although it was better than nothing, these things were by no means reliable and often led to illness, infection, or inflammation. It wasn't until 1928 that German physician Ernst Gräfenberg came up with a dependable IUD. Made of a copper coil, users suffered far fewer side effects and pregnancy was rare.

Cover That Thing, Why Don'tcha?

Both the Romans and the Egyptians occasionally used some sort of sheath as a prophylactic, but since then, condoms were invented at least twice more. Both times the idea originated with physicians looking for a way to prevent a wandering penis from catching sexually transmitted diseases rather than as a birth control device. The first documented model is credited to Gabriel Fallopius, who made a small covering that fit over the tip of the penis and required foreskin to hold it in place. This was during the mid-1500s. Covers for circumcised men appeared shortly thereafter. They fit over the entire penis and were tied onto the base with a ribbon. Not only did they have to be washed between uses, they were made of waxed linen which, as you can imagine, put a bit of the kibosh on the man's sensation. They weren't exactly popular.

Fast forward to England a century later. King Charles II was porking everyone in sight. Charged with protecting the horny king from syphilis, his doctor invented a covering for the royal penis made of oiled sheep intestine. Because the sheep gut was very thin, it enjoyed far more popularity than Fallopius's overcoat.

By the late 1800s, companies were manufacturing condoms made of rubber (thus, the nickname "rubbers").

In 1873, American, Anthony Comstock, leader of Comstock's Society for the Suppression of Vice, pushed a bill through Congress that actually made it illegal to use the U.S. Postal System to distribute contraceptive devices and even birth control literature. This law was broadly interpreted to mean contraceptives and/or promoting the concept of birth control was immoral.

Some 40 years later, Comstock's law met up with some vigorous opposition in the form of Margaret Sanger. An early feminist, Sanger felt women should have control over their own childbearing. Having too many babies often wreaked havoc with some women's health, not to mention the physical, financial, and emotional burden. Some turned to abortionists (mostly female, and medically untrained) and often died of complications as a result. Sanger saw birth control as a sane, safe alternative. She fought for birth control in the political arena and defied the law while waiting for the government to come to its senses.

Comstock wanted to nail Sanger's ass to the wall. In 1915, he sent one of his "suppression of vice" agents to ask Margaret's husband for a copy of *Family Limitation*, a birth control pamphlet she had written. This was not an unusual request, and William Sanger complied. A month later, Comstock himself appeared at the Sangers' door to arrest Margaret. Wily one that she was, Margaret had already left for Europe to avoid prosecution, so Comstock arrested William instead. Margaret returned to lend support to her beleaguered hubby and was put on trial herself. Comstock died during William's trial, and when hundreds of Sanger supporters wrote to President Wilson, the prosecutor gave the whole thing up.

As a result (and much to the dismay of the Catholic Church), the government stepped out of the business of preventing the prevention of babies.

Oh, Cut It Out!

Physicians performed vasectomies as early as the 1600s in England. But, as is true with any surgery at the time, it was quite risky. Needless to say, men weren't lining up to be snipped. Women, on the other hand, had suffered major surgery for years in an effort to stop procreation. From complete hysterectomies to tubal ligations, women have long been going under the knife. The relatively simple (and now easily reversible) vasectomy has only become popular in the past decade, mostly because of unwarranted fear and stigma. Even today, many men refuse to entertain the idea.

My Uterus is Falling! My Uterus is Falling!

In the midst of the Victorian Era when ladies didn't speak of such things, apparently ladies spoke of such things—because many of them found out about pessaries. These contraptions were available at drugstores everywhere and were supposed to prevent or help a condition called "prolapsed uterus" (which is basically when a uterus collapses). Made of anything from cotton to wood, these pessaries were inserted into the vagina and, despite what the packaging said, worked as diaphragms. Unless uteruses were collapsing by the thousands, women quickly spread the word that pessaries made fine birth control devices.

Phew!

Today, birth control no longer relies on the haphazard side effects of gizmos and gadgets any more than it relies on a croc-
odiles' constitution. From condoms to the pill, methods of
preventing pregnancy are easy to obtain and for the most part
inexpensive. Today, health officials invariably recommend condoms for sex except in long-term monogamous relationships
because of the plethora of sexually transmitted diseases.

POP QUIZ

QUESTIONS *(Answers start on page 31.)*

1. If a man was caught committing adultery with a married woman in Massachusetts in 1631, he could be
   A. given the death penalty
   B. castrated
   C. severely whipped in public
   D. forced to offer his services as a slave to the woman's husband
   E. toasted by the members of the American Men's Association for Sexual Freedom

2. In New England during the 1700s, an unmarried couple caught fornicating
   A. could receive a 20-year prison term
   B. were almost always exiled from the community
   C. could be whipped or fined, or both
   D. were immediately brought before a judge to be married
   E. were considered animals and had to sleep out in the barn

3. What did the word "bundling" refer to in eighteenth cen-
   tury New England?
   A. the practice of allowing unmarried couples to sleep in
      the same bed as long as they were fully clothed, usually
      with a board between them
   B. the custom of bathing and wrapping a bride in sheer
      linen the morning of her wedding
   C. dried herbs that were tied together and placed inside a
      newlywed couple's mattress to increase fertility
   D. necking
   E. a baby born out of wedlock

4. Intense female bonding was common and accepted in the
   nineteenth century and sometimes crossed the line into the
   realm of the erotic. At Vassar College in the late 1800s if
   a woman took an interest in another, she might pursue her
   in ways that mirrored courting practices. Once the object
   of her affection capitulated, the couple spent all their time
   together. Students used the following term to describe the
   pursuer:
   A. conked
   B. nothing (Women didn't go to college at that time.)
   C. stoned
   D. he-she
   E. smashed

5. In 1948, there were only two states that didn't have laws
   against sodomy, but considered adultery a crime. They
   were
   A. Maine and Texas

B. Vermont and New Hampshire
C. New York and Oregon
D. Utah and Rhode Island
E. Montana and Wyoming

6. In 1968 more than 100 women gathered outside the Miss America pageant to protest
   A. the pageant itself
   B. the all-male judging panel
   C. the disqualification of one of the contestants on the basis that she was on the pill
   D. the rule that said the contestants couldn't be on the pill
   E. the swimsuit portion of the contest

7. The condom is thought to have gotten its name from
   A. the town where the first ones were manufactured
   B. a prostitute who used them
   C. the Earl of Condom
   D. a Latin word meaning lack of feeling
   E. the owner of a brothel who insisted the clients wear them

8. The famous lover Casanova used the following as birth control
   A. a coin
   B. a lemon
   C. champagne
   D. early withdrawal
   E. a thin wire

9. The first version of the pill was made of synthetic hormones derived from
   A. peanuts
   B. sheep ovaries
   C. male ejaculations
   D. wheat germ
   E. yams

10. Before Margaret Sanger, the founder of Planned Parenthood, began her fight to bring birth control options to American women she was
    A. employed as a maternity nurse
    B. a philosophy student
    C. a housemother at a women's college
    D. pregnant at least 14 times
    E. a well-known artist

11. Malcolm X shined shoes at a dance hall in the 1930s. He also frequently
    A. made extra money by reporting white women who left the dance hall with black men
    B. procured black women for white men
    C. sold condoms
    D. sold porno magazines
    E. all of the above

12. In 1953, Kinsey published *Sexual Behavior in the Human Female.* What percentage of the women interviewed admitted to masturbating?
    A. four percent
    B. sixty-two percent

C. seventy-nine percent
D. eighty-four percent
E. ninety-one percent

13. Of the following, which aphrodisiac works?
    A. oysters
    B. ginseng
    C. powdered rhinoceros horn
    D. bull testicles
    E. Spanish Fly

ANSWERS

1. A. given the death penalty
   These people weren't into fooling around. Massachusetts enacted the death penalty for adultery between a man and a married woman.

2. C. could be whipped or fined, or both
   After their punishment, and if they seemed truly repentant, they were forgiven and easily assimilated back into the community. It was not unusual for men who had been accused of improper advances or consentual sex to achieve positions of respect. For engaged couples caught fornicating, the fines were less severe.

3. A. the practice of allowing unmarried couples to sleep in the same bed as long as they were fully clothed, usually with a board between them
   Most homes did not have a guest room, so when a man

visited his intended, the couple often slept together. To prevent any sexual activity, usually a bundling board was placed between them.

4. E. smashed

5. B. Vermont and New Hampshire

6. A. the pageant itself
Feminists felt the contest was degrading and made sex objects out of women. They felt that women were enslaved by the trappings of the pageant, such as bras, girdles, false eyelashes, makeup, etc., and that the contest was held for male gratification.

7. C. the Earl of Condom
Although he reputedly invented the condom for his patient, King Charles II, the earl hated the fact that the device became known by his name.

8. B. a lemon
Casanova often gave his lovers a partially squeezed lemon half, which they used as a cervical cap. It was fairly effective because it not only created a physical block, the lemon juice acted as a spermicide.

9. E. yams
Chemistry Professor Russell Marker was experimenting with plants in the jungles of Mexico when he discovered that yams put through a series of chemical processes would yield synthetic progesterone. The rest, as they say, is history.

10. A. employed as a maternity nurse
It was at her job that Sanger first realized how many unwanted babies were being born and how often women were seeking abortions with botched results.

11. C. sold condoms

12. B. sixty-two percent

13. Trick question! Although all these things have been touted as aphrodisiacs, there is no research to support that any of them work. The infamous Spanish Fly, which is made from ground beetles, enjoyed immense popularity but caused more than a few unsuspecting women to become violently ill. It was supposed to cause uncontrollable horniness in a woman who swallowed it so it was surreptitiously added to more than a few cocktails. While it didn't produce a willing partner, it could cause bladder irritation, ulcers, diarrhea, and even death.

2

TO CENSOR
OR NOT TO CENSOR

NOOKIE, AND NAVELS, AND NIPPLES—OH MY!

From a titillating glimpse of a woman's ankle to no-holds-barred fetish sites on the Internet, sex and the American media have a long and tumultuous history. Lucky for us, there are always some righteous folks out there who work tirelessly to keep us from the dangers of coming into contact with obscene material. They have censored and banned, then fought innumerable battles in the judicial system to protect us from sights and sounds they've deemed offensive. But that pesky old Constitution keeps getting in the way.

Obscenity is largely subject to opinion, and statutes on the subject use words like "immoral" and "objectionable," which tend to raise arguments rather than define guidelines.

Toward the end of the 1800s, for instance, romance novels

became popular. The genre was
quickly denounced because it
promoted the idea of romantic

> *Is sex dirty? Only if it's done right.*
> —WOODY ALLEN

marriage, which supposedly led to lascivious thoughts, promoted lust, and aroused passion. Victorian attitudes dictated
that the mere idea of physical attraction (obviously the basis of
a "love" marriage) was considered objectionable. A generation
later, marriages based on love had become acceptable. Romance novels (at least those without any sexual references),
although not respected, were no longer considered obscene.
Today, romance novels are thought of as rather innocuous.

By the turn of the century, movies had made their debut
and stirred up the self-appointed guardians of American souls.
At first, it was glimpses of bare ankle that incensed the virtuous.
Anything to do with birth control was also totally taboo. As
time marched on and hemlines went up, ankles were a moot
point, but the belly button was definitely a no-show. Midway
through the twentieth century, birth control came out of the
dark and right into the spotlight of controversy.

Once the navel was revealed, the nipple became the big no-
no. A naked nipple still cannot be seen on network TV but
can easily be found on cable.

The fervor to keep straight sex out of the media was eventually replaced with trying to keep homosexual sex out of the
media.

When the watchful find something to censor, there has almost always been an advocate for freedom of speech to argue
the point.

THAT ORIFICE HAS BEEN OSTRACIZED!

As late as the 1950s, oral and anal sex were widely considered acts of sexual perversion and could result in prosecution. Although some municipalities still have laws against such activities, they are rarely invoked. These laws were originally passed by homophobic folks who wanted to keep their fellow countrymen as straight as possible. But the laws were occasionally used against not only straight couples, but even married couples.

Nowadays, a blow job is hardly considered perverted but when it is given by a man, homophobia still rears (no pun intended) its ugly head. Jerry Falwell, that ever-vigilant defender of morals, went into a tizzy over Teletubby Tinky Winky, claiming the character promoted homosexuality. As proof, Falwell cited Tinky Winky's color (purple, apparently a gay color), the triangle on Tink's head (apparently a gay shape), and the fact that Tinky carries a purse (apparently a clue to sexual preference).

Since the Teletubbies are unlikely to appeal to anyone over the age of three-and-a-half, it is interesting that Falwell thinks the audience sophisticated enough to pick up on these subtle suggestions and be influenced by them some ten to fifteen years later when it is time to start dating.

"THAT'S DISGUSTING! IMMORAL! FILTHY!" "EXCELLENT! LET'S RAISE THE PRICE!"

Books, photos, films, songs, and even comic books have been dragged into court for everything from mild innuendo to entire themes. Occasionally, the whole process can get a bit skewed.

Some groups, such as a local school board voting to ban a book from their curriculum, have been known to censor something, not based on the actual work, but on a description of the work and/or pieces of the work taken out of context. Not so surprising, this type of censorship usually ends up in court pretty quickly.

The most powerful censorship, however, often has nothing to do with the legal system. After all, 'tis money that makes the world go 'round. Catholic leaders in the '50s and '60s, for instance, influenced the content of films and television by promoting mass boycotts. Many movie producers and television sponsors, afraid to incur a boycott, censored their material accordingly.

Since then, however, consumers have turned the tide. There's gold in them there tales of sex, and some entertainers—like "shock jock" Howard Stern and talk-show host Jerry Springer—have mined that gold for both themselves and their sponsors. Stern delights fans and appalls adversaries with his irreverent and hilarious discussions of sex, while Springer's appeal could be described more as a sexual side show. But each of them regularly go to the edge, generating both outrage and outrageous income.

THERE'S NOTHING LIKE SNUGGLING IN BED WITH A GOOD BOOK

Before technology could bring us sexual images, we had to imagine them while reading spicy stories. And everyone knows what a crime that is. The Comstock Act of 1873 (See page 24.) gave police the power to arrest anyone caught with "obscene" material. In the 1920s, the police and the courts were very busy

NAUGHTY, NAUGHTY . . . GIRLIE MAGAZINES
OF THE 1950s AND 1960s

Canid	Gent
Consort	Swank
Sextet	Bachelor
Cloud 9	Modern Man
Torrid	Cavalcade
Black Garter	Ace
Rogue	Exclusive
Frolic	Sir
Chicks for Chuckles	

trying to fight that most obscene of pornography, birth control information.

In an effort to eradicate the terrible threat of birth control, practically anything—books, pamphlets, ads for books, etc.— that smacked of preventing pregnancy could end up in a costly court battle. So vigilant were the authorities that a book called *Contraception*, which was a scientific book written specifically for the medical community, was brought into court on obscenity charges in 1931. The book detailed theories, practices, and the history of birth control—information clearly liable to turn the most virtuous doctor into a pervert.

In Massachusetts an obscenity charge against some birth control pamphlets went all the way to the state supreme court. Trial records indicate that the information pamphlets were accused of being "obscene, indecent, and impure of language," but, like many such cases, there are no specifics.

In 1930, one of the first generally accepted "marital manuals"

THOU SHALT NOT READ . . .

A tiny sampling of authors whose books have been banned for sexual content at one time or another

Erskine Caldwell
James Joyce
D. H. Lawrence
William Faulkner
Harold Robbins
Henry Miller
Judy Blume
Mark Twain

was published. *Ideal Marriage*, written by Theodore Van de Velde, assumed that marriage is better if the sex is mutually enjoyed. The book explicitly described foreplay and various coital positions and helped pioneer American acceptance of the female orgasm. Van de Velde probably never imagined the depth and scope of sex manuals that occupy racks of space in today's bookstores.

About this time, pulp romances started appearing. Considered trashy and occasionally hauled into court, these stories merely contained suggestive prose, referring to things such as "a mad love of pleasure," (translation: slut) and "glorious temptations" (translation: feeling horny). By the mid-'40s, the pulps became widely available. The covers were usually lurid and sex was an integral part of the story (although the endings were generally moralistic). Lesbian novels flourished briefly and were popular among gay women and straight men.

Did this mean mentioning the existence of sex was now

acceptable? Well, writers like Henry Miller wouldn't say so. His books were banned in the United States. It's probably more truthful to say this was precursor to the publishing industry's completely ambiguous attitude toward sex during the 1950s.

The Catholic National Organization for Decent Literature had been formed in the late '30s to protect the public from immoral references, wherever they might appear. From books to comics, they hunted down objectionable material and went after the middle men—organizing boycotts and picket lines in front of newsstands, bookstores, and drugstores that carried the offensive stuff. The organization lost steam during and directly after World War II but was back in action in the '50s. In 1952, Congress considered the issue of explicit sex in mainstream printed matter and came to the conclusion that porno led to juvenile delinquency. This deduction, along with general cold war paranoia and McCarthyism, helped spawn a host of committees and "nonsecular" groups dedicated to clogging the courts with obscenity cases and denouncing dangerously immoral literature, such as *Catcher in the Rye*. The Catholic organization, while not officially sanctioned by Congress, had a powerful voice among these committees and groups, not to mention a potent influence among millions of church members. Despite their best efforts, however, they were unable to stop the tidal wave of change that would take place in the '50s and '60s.

With a directly opposing perspective, Hugh Hefner published the first *Playboy* in December 1953. It not only featured nude photos, it promoted the attitude that sex was fun and could be enjoyed by single folks.

The Kinsey Reports, although highly controversial, were still gaining recognition and acceptance in both the scientific and publishing world. One thing was becoming abundantly clear:

YOU'VE GOT TO BE KIDDING

Anyone can raise an objection to a particular book being used in school. If the school board agrees, they can order that the book (or actually, any kind of offensive material) be removed from the curriculum and/or the building and, violà!, the nasty thing has officially been censored.

Now, this actually has nothing to do with sex, but it's a censorship story with a twist so wonderfully ironic, we had to include it:

An administrator at the Mark Twain Intermediate School in Fairfax County, Virginia, objected to one particular book, calling it, "a grotesque example of racism." The author of the offensive book?

Mark Twain!

the moral ideals of the time and the assumption that most people were adhering to those ideals was more rhetorical than true. The Kinsey Reports were scientific evidence of a chasm between the day's rote and its reality.

In San Francisco, Lawrence Ferlinghetti, who owned and operated the bohemian City Lights Bookstore, published Allen Ginsberg's *Howl,* a book-length poem in which he explores his erotic joy of homosexuality in bold and explicit language. In June of 1957, Ferlinghetti was arrested and copies of *Howl* were confiscated, but when the case went to court, the judge ruled that the poem had literary merit. Following the ruling, sex became a common theme in the print media and was easily available to the middle class. But that didn't mean there weren't plenty of objections.

NOW, THAT'S A HAND JOB

In 1934 the question of whether *Ulysses* by James Joyce was obscene came before Judge Augustus Hand in the Second Circuit Court of Appeals.

He ruled that material charged as obscene should be judged in context and the work as a whole should be taken into consideration, rather than banning on the basis of a specific passage. Hand's decision paved the way for courts to narrow the definition of obscenity and make allowances for artistic expression.

Former Grove Press owner Barney Rosset went to court time and again in the 1960s for publishing books such as *Naked Lunch, Tropic of Cancer,* and *Lady Chatterly's Lover.* Now considered classics, each of these books has erotic passages that were charged as obscene. Rosset won his cases on the basis of the First Amendment.

By 1966, the Supreme Court had been redefining the parameters of obscenity so regularly that when they heard a case against *Fanny Hill,* they ruled that unless a book was "utterly without redeeming social value" it could not be considered obscene. This ruling, along with rapidly changing social mores, paved the way for substantial public tolerance toward sex in the print media. Magazines such as *Penthouse* and *Screw* (although not without their own fights) became widely available.

In the early 1960s Helen Gurley Brown's *Sex and the Single Girl* was a runaway hit. In it, Brown promoted sex as a powerful weapon for women, as well as a pleasurable pastime. The book represented a new attitude and a new direction in pub-

SEE NO EVIL!

Ratings from the Catholic Legion of Decency in the 1960s

A-1 = Morally unobjectionable for general patronage
A-2 = Morally unobjectionable for adults and adolescents
A-3 = Morally unobjectionable for adults
A-4 = Morally objectionable for adults, with reservations
 B = Morally objectionable in part for all
 C = Condemned

lishing. Erotic novels and sex manuals soon became staples on the best-seller list.

Publishers and authors are still called into court on occasion, but book banning today is more about barring material from libraries and/or schools than about legal ramifications. Some issues that have led to modern book bannings (or attempts) have been a children's book about a family with same-sex parents, and a young adult novel that includes an abortion scene. Although these books have won highly respected literary awards and are not obscene in any judicial sense, some communities have chosen to restrict them from communal access.

OF COURSE, THE VISUAL ARTS ARE QUITE ENTERTAINING

While publishers were fighting for the First Amendment, the film and television industries were navigating their own path through the seas of censorship.

ALL THAT PORNO WILL TURN YOU INTO A MANIAC!!

Does pornography warp people?

In 1970, The Commission of Obscenity and Pornography (established by President Johnson) found that sexual behaviors are, for the most part, very stable and not particularly altered by watching pornography.

In fact, studies have shown that many sex offenders (such as rapists and child molesters) were, on average, exposed to less pornography as adolescents than their peers.

Denmark legalized hardcore pornography in 1965 and subsequently reported a reduction in the number of sex crimes.

The exception to this is violent pornography. Research has repeatedly shown that watching graphic depictions of violent sexual behavior increases aggression and decreases empathy.

In 1986, a commission established by Attorney General Edwin Meese concluded that pornography leads to violence, but closer inspection reveals that the study discounted any evidence to the contrary. Because of bias, the study, and its conclusion, wasn't very scientific.

By 1921, the movies, which had become quite sensual, were commonly blamed for the collapse of morals in the United States, although in fact, films were reflecting them—and belatedly at that. (The fast and loose Jazz Age was already in full swing.) Some folks were calling for laws to stem the tide of horniness. So, the industry hired Republican politician Will Hays to clean up Hollywood's image and avoid the threat of

MAGAZINES FOR TODAY'S READER

There's a Whip in My Valise
Do It with Your Shoes On
Encyclopedia Sexualis
Yesterday's Porno
100% Real Wives
Naughty Neighbors
Pledges and Paddles
Men in Uniform
A Guide to the Correction of Young Gentlemen
Boot Lover's Digest
Cruella's Goddess
Knotty
Fighting Females

government censorship. Hays and his people (commonly referred to as the Hays Office) developed The Hays Code (commonly referred to as The Code) in 1934. It was a list of 11
"don'ts" and 27 "be carefuls" that served as guidelines to keep
objectionable scenes and references out of films. That same
year, the Catholic Church formed the Legion of Decency,
which created the first movie ratings. The Catholic ratings had
enough clout to affect the financial success of a movie, so filmmakers quickly began adhering to the Code and working with
the legion to ensure a good rating. For some reason, comedy
had its own rules, so that Mae West or the Marx Brothers could
get away with innuendoes that would never have been toler-
ated in drama. And censors allowed adultery and premarital sex
within the context of a story line as long as the participant got

"punished" for his or her behavior. A Hollywood wit once pointed out that to please the censors the hero and heroine had to remain chaste and the villain could have tons of fun and lots of sex—"you just have to shoot him in the end." Not surprisingly, films of the era saw an increase in violence as entertainment as moviemakers began to rely on gangsters to titillate the viewing public.

As was true with the Catholic literature organization, the Legion of Decency lost a lot of its power following World War II, and movies began to push the edge of what was acceptable. The introduction of television into American homes also had a tremendous impact on what was seen in the movies. The motive was money and competition was fierce. Sponsors dictated a clean, all-American image on television shows, so some filmmakers got bolder, partly in the hopes of attracting attention. Howard Hughes created enormous debate with *The Outlaws*. Starring Jane Russell (or at least starring Jane Russell's sumptuous breasts), *The Outlaws* was basically a fairly bad movie filled with shots of Russell's cleavage spilling out of extremely low-cut clothes. The censors were appalled—they even blew their corks over the advertisement posters for the movie. But Hughes, who had directed the picture, had both the tenacity and the money to wage war against censorship. When the film was released amid controversy, the movie industry learned a lasting lesson: Bad publicity equals good box office returns.

But while Hughes was pushing the edge of the envelope (or edge of the bodice, as it were), most directors were staying well within the limits of The Code. Again, the motive was money. If a film followed The Code, it received the Seal of Approval. Those films released without a seal had a much more difficult time making money, especially since many religious leaders called on their congregations to not only boycott but also to picket theaters daring to run films without a seal.

In both movies and television, married couples shown in bedroom scenes were usually in twin beds. If a couple was shown in a double bed, then at least one of them would have at least one foot on the floor. This was so common that even some producers believed it was dictated by The Code, although that's not true. It was, however, an easy way for producers and directors to know for sure they would not have to reshoot a bedroom scene to satisfy the censors.

In the '50s, obscenity charges against films were very common, but many had to do with foreign and/or underground films. (For a while, Hollywood did its best not to corrupt American youth, but then simply couldn't help itself.) Then, *A Streetcar Named Desire* came out and fought and won a big censorship milestone. The film deals with two topics—homosexuality and rape—that sent some people scurrying to charge the filmmakers with obscenity. But the court ruled in favor of *Streetcar.*

Elia Kazan, director of *Streetcar,* shot a scene for *Splendor in the Grass* (1961) that showed a nude Natalie Wood running down a hall from the back. It was the first time a movie aimed at a general audience contained such a scene. The censors had a fit, as did the Legion of Decency, and Kazan cut the scene. But change was in the wind.

For one thing, there was a certain amount of preposterousness in some of the censorship. Take, for example, the female navel. Branded as too indecent for film at some point, belly buttons could be seen on any American beach by the late '50s. And an early Cleopatra movie featured a starlet wearing a gauzy skirt and nothing but a few jewels on her nipples. But a remake in the '60s with Elizabeth Taylor caused a major problem because her navel showed. At first the director had animators erase Taylor's navel, but it looked way too weird. They eventually solved the problem by sticking a jewel into it. The absurdity did not go unnoticed.

Some Hollywood producers were shooting two versions of their films, one for Europe; one for the United States. Some producers were choosing not to belong to the Motion Picture Association and therefore didn't have to submit their movies for censorship review. Their pictures were turning a tidy profit and European films shown at "art" houses were also generating quite a bit of cash. It soon became too much money for legitimate Hollywood to ignore.

By the end of the '60s, navels seemed a moot point. *I Am Curious—Yellow* is a Swedish movie from 1969 that was seized and censored when it came into the United States, but the case came before the Supreme Court, which ruled in favor of the First Amendment. *I Am Curious* was rated *X* for nudity and graphic sex scenes. The plot mixed radical sex with radical politics and made scads of money. A movie whose time had come, *I Am Curious—Yellow* proved a landmark case for a now thriving sex industry. With stage productions like *Hair* and *Oh! Calcutta!* (which featured live nudity and focused on sex) playing on Broadway, it was increasingly hard for censors in Hollywood to stick to their outdated Code.

Smart entrepreneurs capitalized on the growing trend of open sexuality. Movies like *Deep Throat, The Devil in Miss Jones,* and *Last Tango in Paris* (featuring respected actor Marlon Brando) became almost mainstream and could be viewed at many local theaters across the country. But even the most liberal anticensorship champions could balk on occasion. In the mid-1970s an underground movie called *Snuff* caused quite a controversy. In it, a woman is gutted, then cut into pieces. It was rumored that the woman had actually been killed during the filming. The rumor was untrue, but the idea that a sado-masochistic film could actually end in death proved to be more than most could take. Movies catering to distasteful fetishes (such as those that involve killing, eating excrement, or abusing children) existed pretty far underground and out of sight from middle America. This has changed with the Internet, but more about that later.

Permissiveness on television wasn't moving nearly as quickly as in other media in the '60s. It was quite an event when Barbara Eden bared her belly button on the sitcom *I Dream of Jeannie*. Of course, once that was allowed, navels could be seen all over TV. Beginning with double entendres and sexual innuendoes, network television slowly started getting racier. One of the first television genres to take advantage of the public's avid interest in sex-as-entertainment was the afternoon soap opera.

By the early '80s, home video players and cable television were giving both the television and the film industry some stiff (oops, no pun intended) competition. They responded by making some of their own products sexier. Network television eased up on restrictions more and more, so that by the mid-1990s, the naked behinds of the *NYPD Blue* stars could be found on a fairly regular basis. Previously unheard words (such as "bitch") started showing up in the course of ordinary television dialog. Mariel Hemingway kissed Roseanne on the mouth on a sitcom. Needless to say, for some it seemed television was now the devil's toy. But interestingly, two of the biggest controversies of recent television were about concepts—

AT THIS RATE, THEY'LL NEVER HAVE SEX

Networks now rate many of their shows. They take sex, violence, and adult situations and language into consideration. The ratings are

TV-Y	Appropriate for children as young as preschool
TV-G	Appropriate for general audiences
TV-PG	Parental guidance suggested
TV-14	Not recommended for viewers under 14
TV-M	For mature audiences only

when Candice Bergen's title character on *Murphy Brown* decided to have a baby out of wedlock; and when Ellen Degeneres's character on *Ellen* openly admitted she was gay—not about nudity or language.

Despite what some would consider a too-liberal policy about sex on television, the United States lags behind many other countries, particularly those in Europe. It's the power of the dollar. Networks compete with videos and cable for viewers. And while some viewers prefer no censorship, others demand more restrictions. Fearing government involvement, the TV industry scrambled for a solution. Enter the V-chip and television ratings. The V-chip allows parents to program their sets to prevent receiving objectionable broadcasts. (Although some say that since many kids are far more techno-savvy than their parents, the V-chip is more adultproof than childproof.) Television ratings are used by most of the networks and some of the cable stations. Most networks aim to get a TV-G rating for their prime-time shows. This is an opposition to films, for

PICTURE THAT

In the 1980s, artist Robert Mapplethorpe caused a major public outcry with a traveling exhibit of his photographs. Although many people objected to the homoerotic nature of the pictures, it was the fact that the exhibit was financed by the National Endowment for the Arts that gave objectors a voice. The NEA was already under fire by conservative Republicans for helping finance a magazine called *Gay Sunshine Press*.

The result of the uproar was legislation allowing Congress to place limits on the content of art when sponsored by tax dollars.

which producers don't particularly want a G rating, because in movies a G generally translates to kid's programming.

Much rating is actually quite subjective. Obviously, explicit sex is not going to allow for a PG rating, but the distinction between R and NC-17 is blurry. An R translates to much better receipts at the box office; NC-17 suggests a film verging on pornography. But each could contain the same amount of footage with the same amount of exposed flesh and indecent activity and not get the same rating.

THE SOUND OF MUSIC MADE BY SINNERS

It didn't start with naughty rock-and-roll lyrics. Verdi's operas (for political reasons) and a ballet of Bartok's (for themes of prostitution and erotic content) were subject to the censors of their time. And during the first half of the twentieth century, it wasn't unusual for songs to be banned from the radio. For instance, "Frankie and Johnnie," an old folk song, wasn't allowed because within the tale it mentions that Frankie and Johnnie visit a prostitute. So, okay, content is one thing. But in the '40s, some songs were prohibited from the airwaves that didn't even have words! The problem, it seems, is that their titles were suggestive. Two examples are "Dirty Lady" and "Lavender Cowboy."

A tide of sexuality washed over America with the advent of rock and roll. Everyone knows about Elvis's hip-shaking, morality-breaking stage presence. But that was only the start of what would get the censors' panties in a bunch. By the '60s, some bands got around the censors with a nod and a wink— for instance, Mick Jagger's tongue-in-cheek reference to a honky-tonk woman who blows his "nose." Other bands didn't bother (such as Country Joe and the Fish, who spelled out the word "fuck" in one of their hits). But censorship in music didn't really become an issue until Tipper Gore and her cronies brought it to the forefront in 1986 by demanding record labeling. Controversy over labeling has gone on since. Nirvana's album, *In Utero,* was at the center of a turning point in 1993. The CD featured a fetus on the cover and a song entitled "Rape Me." Partly in response to consumer pressure, some mass-marketing chains, including WalMart, Kmart, and Target, refused to carry the CD. Six months later, Geffen Records (the producers of *In Utero*), feeling the sting of commercial censorship, changed the song title and the cover art to get into these markets. The dollar triumphs again! Most recording companies now label albums containing objectionable lyrics, and many of today's recording artists now produce two versions of the same songs—one suitable for airplay and sales in mass-market stores, the other with original lyrics.

But even in music there is occasional curious censorship. In 1995, Paula Abdul's "Crazy Cool" video was nixed by MTV censors for suggestive dance moves. Abdul was reportedly mystified by the ruling but complied voluntarily. The banning is curious in light of other videos allowed by the censors (such as Michael Jackson's crotch-grabbing dances). But such is the changing tide of censorship.

POP QUIZ

QUESTIONS *(Answers start on page 57.)*

1. In 1988, the national syndicate that distributes the *Jerry Springer Show* yanked an episode at the last minute, presumably because it was too tasteless. The name of the episode was
   A. "Women Who Are Whipping Posts."
   B. "I Like to Bathe with the Baby."
   C. "I Married a Horse."
   D. "Fellows Who Like Feces."

2. *Cult of the Spankers, Trailer Trollop,* and *$20 Lust* are all
   A. titles of pulp books from the 1940s
   B. titles of porno movies from the 1950s
   C. titles of various Montel Williams shows from the 1990s
   D. names of underground sex clubs in New York

3. In 1929, a book entitled *The Well of Loneliness* was censored for being perverted. It was censored because

A. one of its characters masturbates;

B. a lesbian affair is described in it;

C. the author alludes to the sexual feelings of a priest;

D. it was actually a guide to sexual fetishes.

4. Some New York newsdealers lost their licenses in 1951 for selling which of the following?
   A. *Epidermis*
   B. *A Gynecologist's Guide to the City*
   C. *A Man's Man*
   D. *Hygiene for Health*

5. In the 1960s, Masters and Johnson published a book entitled *Human Sexual Response*. The book shocked a lot of people because
   A. it reported that most women will respond to sexual stimulation, even if the stimulation comes from another woman;
   B. it reported that most men will respond to sexual stimulation, even if the stimulation comes from another man;
   C. researchers gathered some of their material by observing actual sexual activities of the volunteers;
   D. Masters and Johnson had sex with nearly half the subjects involved in the study.

6. The Motion Picture Association of America started its own rating system in
   A. 1968
   B. 1969
   C. 1970
   D. 1972

7. In 1998, Ted Turner made a decision regarding the films running on his cable station Turner Classic Movies (TMC). That decision was to
   A. start his own rating system, which even takes bad role modeling such as drug scenes into consideration
   B. cut all offensive scenes and language from the films
   C. stop airing R-rated movies
   D. air movies uncut, including R-rated ones

8. In the late 1990s, several films given R ratings contained scenes previously barred by the ratings board. What was seen in the scenes that was previously thought of as obscene?
   A. a penis
   B. a vagina
   C. a homosexual act
   D. an act of sadomasochism

9. Kevin Bacon's penis can be seen very briefly in
   A. *Gomorra*
   B. *Boogie Nights*
   C. *Wild Things*
   D. *Wild Nights*
   E. *Seven Days*

10. In 1998, the Catholic League for Religious and Civil Rights had a nearly successful boycott against a prime-time show because of the way the show portrayed a priest. The show that caused such a fervor was
    A. *Nothing Sacred*
    B. *King of the Hill*

C. *20/20*

D. *Seventh Heaven*

11. A record-store owner was convicted on obscenity charges for selling a censored CD of the band 2 Live Crew in what state?

    A. Ohio

    B. Florida

    C. Utah

    D. Texas

12. There is a law in California obligating photo labs to report pornographic pictures of children to authorities. True or false

ANSWERS

1. C. "I Married a Horse."

2. A. titles of pulp books from the 1940s

3. B. A lesbian affair is described in it.

4. D. *Hygiene for Health.*
   Hygiene for Health, Sunshine and Health, Sunbathing for Health, and *Modern Sunbathing* are all titles of nudist magazines of the '50s.

5. C. Researchers gathered some of their material by observing actual sexual activities of the volunteers.

6. A. 1968 (It was November of 1968 that the Motion Picture Association first started rating movies.)

7. C. to stop airing R-rated movies
   At first Turner tried to edit out offensive scenes, but was highly criticized because the cutting interfered with the integrity of so many films. Turner decided to stop offering movies that had R ratings rather than show them uncut.

8. A. a penis

9. C. *Wild Things*
   Toward the end of the film, Bacon steps out of a shower and there is a quick, full-frontal nude flash before he wraps a towel around himself.

10. A. *Nothing Sacred*
    Although some Catholics supported the show, the official church view was dim. They didn't care for the portrayal of the church or the priest, especially when he had—omigosh—sexual feelings.

11. B. Florida

12. True

3

CAN'T BUY ME LOVE

Maybe money can't buy you love—but let's take a look at what it *can* buy you.

The "world's oldest profession" has a long and colorful history dating back before the

> *If prostitution continues so, and the main classes of young men immerse themselves more and more in it . . . what will be the result?*
> —WALT WHITMAN, 1857

birth of Jesus Christ. Seems as long as men have had penises and a sex drive, they've wanted to pay women to have sex with them. Ramses II, in the thirteenth century B.C., for instance, had five or six favorite wives, over one hundred children, and a large harem of slave-girl prostitutes who eventually conspired to kill him. Ramses apparently had trouble keeping all those women satisfied. Young upper-class boys growing up in Ramses' time could use household slave-girl prostitutes as they saw fit. However, outside of harems, prostitutes could ac-

---

DICK-SHUN-ARY

In old English, the word "whore" means desire.

---

tually earn money for their trade. From Mary Magdalene to modern-day hookers and call girls, exchanging sex for money is as old as time.

IT'S ALL GREEK TO ME

"Pornoi" is Greek for whore, and the Greeks seemed to find prostitutes fascinating. Their wives were less fortunate. Apparently Greek men believed in that old adage of leaving the little woman at home. Greek women were often confined to home and the tending of children. They had little or no public life. Greek men did not take their wives with them to visit their friends or business acquaintances. Their wives didn't get to go to parties. Or the market. As a matter of fact, they didn't get to do much of anything. This splitting off of wives from society meant that the only women many Greeks encountered besides their wives were prostitutes. Prostitutes weren't locked away. They partied with their clients and got to make money doing so.

Prostitutes in Greek times, as throughout much of history, had levels of status. At the lowest level were those women who worked in brothels. Men paid a small fee to enter a brothel (which was taxed by a type of "hooker collection" bureau) and paid the women they chose with small trinkets and gifts. These women could never accumulate wealth or status. Above these women, but not by much, were the streetwalkers who tried to entice men on the street. No hot pants and platform shoes for these women. Instead they painted "follow me" or other blatant sayings on their sandals. (The dawn of shoe fetishes perhaps? But more on that in the "You Want to Do *What?*" chapter.)

Next up the ladder were prostitutes who could dance, entertain, or play the flute and other instruments. These women could become wealthy if they

> *Sex without love is a meaningless experience, but as meaningless experiences go it's pretty damn good.*
> —WOODY ALLEN

were popular, and Athens even erected a temple to one of them—the Venus Lamia.

At the top of the sexual pyramid were a type of courtesan called hetaerae. These sexual wonders were able to captivate the most important men of Greece and were thus elevated to a high status. They were expected to wear exotic makeup, dress "correctly," and be able to converse intelligently in the company of men. They also got out of the house and probably had a much better time than the poor old Greek wives stuck at home with a pack of kids, a household to run, and no Valium to dull the boredom.

Apparently, hetaerae found their lives preferable to being shut away. Most of them raised their daughters in the ways of hetaerae. Like mother like daughter.

WHEN IN ROME . . .

Romans also had a hierarchy of prostitutes. While courtesans were at the top, Roman wives were allowed out of the house, and therefore the courtesan was not as exalted a position. In

X-RATED MOVIE TITLES

Ejacula
The Bodyguard
Cliff Banger
Foreskin Gump
Passenger 69
A Rear and Pleasant Danger

other words, looking down on prostitutes became fashionable. A sign of things to come.   .

They also didn't wear sandals with sex slogans on them. However, they did have to distinguish themselves from Roman matrons. (Wouldn't want to confuse the town slut with the wife of a senator now, would we?) Prostitutes therefore had to wear short togas, rather than long, to show their "place" in society. Was this the dawn of miniskirts, hot pants, and spike heels? Maybe not, but in an ancient version of "blondes have more fun," prostitutes sometimes even bleached their hair with a form of peroxide to set themselves apart from "regular" women.

In Roman times, male slaves couldn't marry and were kept in households separate from the females. We're talking about a lot of frustrated male slaves! They were, however, allowed to visit brothels as their only form of sexual release. The prostitutes who served these slaves, and those that serviced men in the military service, were on the very bottom rung of the Roman social ladder.

Unlike the modern criminalization of prostitution, Romans thought prostitutes performed a vital community service.

ANOTHER WAY TO SAY "INTERCOURSE"

Bumping uglies
Hiding the salami
Doing the nasty
Hitting a home run
Checking into a womb at Paradise Motel
Sending in the purple-helmeted warrior
Meeting the staff
Evicting the testicular squatters
Disobeying the pope

Though Romans valued the family unit, they felt prostitution must be allowed to help curb the sexual appetites of men. In an ancient version of "boys will be boys" thinking, the Romans reasoned that if men went to brothels, they were less likely to have an affair with another man's wife.

SAINT'S ALIVE

Mary Magdalene was a former prostitute who counted Jesus Christ as her friend. Most have heard of her, but how about Saint Mary the Harlot? Legend has it that the young Mary lived

> *When authorities warn you of the sinfulness of sex, there is an important lesson to be learned. Do not have sex with the authorities.*
>
> —MATT GROENING

with her uncle, a hermit named Abraham. She prayed with her uncle and followed his holy ways. However, one of her uncle's friends, a young monk, began to pay attention to the beautiful

X-RATED MOVIE TITLES
White Men Can Hump
Bone Alone
The Cable Girl
Frisky Business
Honey, I Blew Everybody
Howard Sperm's Private Parties

Mary. She lost her virginity to him in a rush of passion and then, realizing her status as a "fallen" woman, ran away to join a brothel. (Logical, right?)

Abraham looked for her for a couple of years and eventually found her by disguising himself as a soldier in need of servicing. Mary made a play for her uncle (who, for some reason, she did not recognize), but in a fit of remorse, told this "soldier" her life story and how she had become a prostitute. Her uncle revealed his true identity and asked her to leave with him and make amends to God. Mary did and was so faithful in her prayers that she had the power to heal the sick. After her death, Mary the Harlot was made a saint.

GIMME SOME OF THAT OLD-TIME RELIGION

The Jimmy Swaggart and Jim Bakker sex scandals captivated the news media at the time they occurred. However, men and religion and sex have long been intricately interwoven. One of the best examples of religion and sexual hypocrisy was the early Crusades.

ANOTHER WAY TO SAY "THE BOY IS MASTURBATING"

Wanking the willie
Choking the chicken
Jerking the gerkin
Playing pocket pool
Flogging the bishop
Pickle party
Pud pulling
Buffing the banana
A date with DiPalma
Whippin' up on skippy
Flogging the infidel
Spanking the monkey

On pilgrimages during the First Crusade, women "pilgrims" sold sex to pay their way. Sexiness is next to godliness, perhaps? Prostitutes set up camps near the pilgrims' camps as well. And, if the leaders of a certain pilgrimage tried to oust these women, enterprising prostitutes often dressed up as men and rode in disguise. However, these "men's" tents were awfully busy at night. Party hearty, "men."

As time marched on, bringing prostitution along with it, even Saint Thomas Aquinas agreed that if prostitution was rendered illegal, sodomy would become rampant. In a sense, controlled prostitution would keep the world's sexual mores in check. Or so he thought.

During the Fourth Crusade, efforts were made to reform prostitutes. If a man married a reformed prostitute, it was preached that this earned him a gold star with God and helped

DICK-SHUN-ARY

The word "fuck" originated from the Old English *fokken,* which meant "to beat against."

It wasn't considered crude until the Normans invaded England. Thinking themselves superior, the ruling Normans designated many of the words and phrases of the native Anglo-Saxons as coarse. "Fornicate" became the polite replacement.

Fornicate has been traced to the latin *fornix,* meaning a basement room with a high ceiling. In a classic old case of verbing a noun, prostitutes often plied their trade in a fornix, which became a description of the act.

the man's chances of getting into heaven. For a time, the Church even offered a financial incentive to each man who married a reformed harlot. Gold stars, a slut for a wife, *and* money, how could men resist?

Throughout time and doctrine, Christians have had mixed feelings about prostitutes, reformed prostitutes, and sex in general. In the 1400s, if a Christian had sex with a Jewish prostitute, the Jewish woman could be burned alive. However, like most periods of history, the "john" was unpunished. Most likely because it was the men who made the rules.

Love is the answer, but while you are waiting for the answer, sex raises some pretty good questions.

—WOODY ALLEN

By the time Puritans were migrating to the New World, religious men advocated all kinds of punishment for loose women. One Puritan author wrote that women who worked as prostitutes should be

ANOTHER WAY TO SAY "THE GIRL IS MASTURBATING"

Stroking the pelt
Petting the pussy
One-woman show
Spelunking without a partner
Going to work without a staff
Beating around the bush
Digital manipulation
Rubbing the nubbin
Taking her own temperature
Cleaning the carpet
Gleaming the tube

branded with a hot iron on their cheeks, forehead, and other body parts. Of course, the author did not recommend branding a man's penis.

I'M A YANKEE DOODLE DANDY

Americans in the New World put their own unique spin on prostitution. Native Americans, African Americans, and indentured servants were often enslaved as prostitutes or forced to work in remote frontier towns where few women lived. Many were sent to live and provide sex in rough mining towns. Suicide was rampant as death was preferable to continued work in their forced profession.

In post–Civil War times, western prostitutes worked in dance halls and saloons. Today's porn stars such as Tawny Peaks, Vic-

X-RATED MOVIE TITLES

The Madam's Family
The Naked Bun
When Larry Ate Sally
Titty Slickers
Intercourse with the Vampire
Pulp Friction
Saving Ryan's Privates

toria Paris, Seka, and Christy Canyon have nothing on the "stage" names of these old gals. Back then you could visit Tit Bit, Dutch Jack, and Wicked Alice. What about one Dodge City prostitute with the decidedly unglamorous nickname of Squirrel Tooth Alice? As a profession, prostitutes were called Mary Magdalenes, scarlet ladies, frail sisters, soiled doves, and "our girls." Almost sounds poetic. Today they are called hookers, streetwalkers, ladies of the evening, and whores.

In late eighteenth-century New York, the most famous and well-visited area of prostitution was called "Holy Ground." In the area around Church Street and Vesey Street, the highest-priced prostitutes flourished on property owned by the Episcopal Church. How's that for a way to fill your coffers?

Prostitutes often worked in frenzied bursts. Records of one early twentieth-century brothel indicated a Delancy Street prostitute serviced 58 different men in a three-hour period. That puts a whole new spin on the term "gettin' busy." Others maintained "regulars," sometimes seeing as many as 180 clients per week. That's over 9,000 men per year. We're talking *very* busy.

ANOTHER WAY TO SAY "PENIS"

The little guy with the helmet
Schlong
Peter and his fuzzy pals
The boss
Trouser trout
Pocket pole
One-eyed monster
The brain
Love sausage
Seed spitter
Captain's log

I'LL TAKE WHAT'S BEHIND DOOR NUMBER 2

So what does a modern-day brothel offer its customers?
Though you can go to any city and buy a hooker for an hour
or an evening, ranging from down-and-dirty sex in a car to
high-priced women who will come to your hotel room, Las
Vegas offers legalized prostitution. And the broad range of services they provide would perhaps amaze their ancient Greek
counterparts. A typical "menu" from a Las Vegas brothel includes such interesting items as

- tongue massage
- water sports
- straight French
- reversed half & half (half oral, half intercourse)
- Japanese quickie

- dominance
- lay back
- hot & cold French (oral sex using coffee and ice cubes to alternate sensations while in the woman's mouth)

Aldous Huxley once said that an intellectual is a person who's found one thing that's more interesting than sex. . . .

From whirlpools to whip cream, if you're into it, they provide it. And how 'bout taking home a little souvenir of your night at the ranch? You can choose from a dazzling array of day-old stockings, panties, garter belts, or condoms.

"Look honey, I got you a Vegas T-shirt and this lovely used rubber."

"Aw, sweetheart . . . you shouldn't have."

AROUND THE WORLD

America has its share of runaways lured into working in the sex trade. Pimps ply young women with drugs and beat them into working long, thankless hours for enough drug money to get their next high. America also has its share of call girls who command a high price for their services and lead a different lifestyle entirely. Call girls willing to do the unusual and cater to fetishists can name their price.

Elsewhere around the world, some places offer legal prostitution. And there is also a thriving market in young girls sold by their parents into the darkest and most inhumane conditions imaginable. Their families may believe they are sending their daughters off to the city to work for a family as a domestic

ANOTHER WAY TO SAY "VAGINA"
Peter pocket
Furry folds
Love nest
Tunnel of love
Little man in a boat (clitoris)
Jade gate
Gate to heaven
Jungle
Bearded clam
Quim

servant. Instead they become prisoners until early death from disease and despair.

Thailand boasts one of the biggest sex trades. "Hostess" clubs, live sexual shows, and beaches that offer on-the-spot quickies make it a sexual destination for both men and women. It also has a thriving business in some of the most vicious aspects of child prostitution—a reason it has garnered international criticism and boycotts from several activist groups.

The Philippine "Triangle" also offers party bars and hostess clubs. M. H. Del Pilar Street has ten blocks jam-packed with prostitution. While considered a dangerous area for tourists, it is cheaper to buy a hooker in the Philippines than probably anywhere else in the world.

Amsterdam offers a glimpse at the "other side" of prostitution—a legal business that is regulated. Coffee houses and sex shops are intertwined along its streets. The Wallen is one of the oldest red-light districts in the world.

X-RATED MOVIE TITLES

Sin-a-Matic
Wild Bill's Panty and Girdle Show
Lactomania
Cumback Pussy
Where the Boys Aren't
Dirty Debutantes

Hamburg, Germany also has a large red-light district—with a police station in the center of it to ensure the streets are safe. "Window brothels" place scantily and exotically clad women in their windows so passersby can window-shop before deciding where to party.

Travel packages are offered so Americans can sample sex "around the world in 80 lays."

And don't forget . . . most established brothels now take major credit cards. . . . "It's everywhere you want to be."

POP QUIZ

QUESTIONS *(Answers start on page 76.)*

(Answers start on page 76.)

1. By the mid-1800s, prostitution in New York was an industry with revenues of approximately
   A. $10 million
   B. $3 million
   C. $300,000
   D. $1 million

2. Who was Butt Ender?
   A. the world's first male porn star
   B. a transvestite show girl with a large following in the early 1920s
   C. the pseudonym of the author of a guidebook on brothels in the mid-1800s
   D. the street name of a famous Boston pimp

3. Ancient Babylonian men sometimes had this unusual relationship with prostitutes
   A. They brought home their prostitutes and if the pros-

titutes got along with the wife of the household, the men adopted them as part of the family.

B. They used them as sex therapists.

C. They were allowed to beat them, but only if they tripled their payment.

D. They tickled them and were tickled in return following sex.

4. In Roman times, what were "grave-watchers"?
   A. couples who copulated on graves to honor the dead
   B. streetwalkers
   C. pimps who were always on the look-out for customers for their prostitutes
   D. women who married much older men in hopes of their dying during sex and thereby leaving the women all their money, according to tradition

5. What was one of the special features of the Hindu temple of Samanatha in India?
   A. It is adorned with pictures of naked women.
   B. It is adorned with pictures of naked men.
   C. It is the only Hindu temple erected (no pun intended) to honor a prostitute.
   D. It offered prostitutes to weary travelers.

6. In ancient China, what was *feng-chung-shu?*
   A. a sexual intercourse manual
   B. an intricate sexual position
   C. bestiality
   D. the lowest level of prostitute

7. Jean-Jacques Rousseau, the famous writer and thinker, was obsessed with a prostitute with this unusual characteristic
   A. She had only one nipple.
   B. She had no teeth and was able to orally satisfy him as no other woman had done before.
   C. She had enormous breasts that rested on her thighs when she was sitting.
   D. She had an ample rear end that required two chairs when she sat down.

8. Who were the "White Ladies" of the thirteenth century?
   A. prostitutes who were required to wear white in order to differentiate themselves from "proper" women
   B. reformed prostitutes who became nuns
   C. nuns who left the convent and, because of the stigma of doing so, were forced into brothels
   D. women who performed in taverns and had a side business servicing inn guests and were noted for their very pale skin because of the late hours they kept—they slept all day long and rarely were outside in the sunshine.

9. What happened to Chinese prostitutes past their prime in San Francisco in the mid-1800s?
   A. They were forced to kill themselves.
   B. They were "retired" to brothel retirement homes up the California coast (many of which are now bed-and-breakfasts).
   C. They were married off at auctions where men could buy a wife at rock-bottom prices.

D. They were forced to work in railroad camps as laundresses.

10. In St. Louis, in 1870, what was the Social Evil Ordinance?
    A. The declaration that prostitutes were insane, and therefore could be confined to mental hospitals.
    B. The declaration that prostitutes were possessed and could therefore have exorcisms performed on them.
    C. An attempt to regulate prostitutes by sometimes sending them to a Social Evil Hospital.
    D. A special power given to policemen to whip and "by any means" remove prostitutes from the streets around the churches—up to and including killing the women.

ANSWERS

1. B. $3 million
   Prostitution revenues were exceeded, at that time, only by the garment industry. Apparently, there's lots of money in clothing, whether they're getting put on or taken off.

2. C. the pseudonym of the author of a guidebook on brothels in the mid-1800s
   In it, he claimed there were over 250 brothels in New York City in 1839.

3. B. They used them as sex therapists.
   If a Babylonian male was impotent, he would sometimes turn to prostitutes for treatment that involved having his penis coated in a special oil that contained magnetic iron

ore, which was thought to increase friction during the sex act.

4. B. streetwalkers
These women were also called "night moths" or "strollers."

5. D. It offered prostitutes to weary travelers.
As many as 500 dancing girls provided music for the gods, 24 hours a day. While they were at it, if a male traveler was feeling a little tense or tired, he could avail himself of their prostitution services.

6. A. a sexual intercourse manual

7. A. She had only one nipple.

8. B. reformed prostitutes who became nuns
Pope Gregory IX established the Order of Mary Magdalene specifically for reformed prostitutes. Convents were set up throughout France, for instance, and often received royal financial support.

9. A. They were forced to kill themselves.
Prostitutes past their prime were taken to "hospitals" where they were given a single bowl of rice, a lamp with oil, and a cup of water. These women knew they were brought to these filthy places to die. Usually these women had venereal diseases or otherwise were ill. They were locked in a room until the oil in their lamp ran out. By that time, they were usually dead due to starvation, though some

committed suicide, perhaps through hanging. If they were still alive after the oil lamp burned out, they were murdered.

10. C. An attempt to regulate prostitutes by sometimes sending them to a Social Evil Hospital.

St. Louis tried to regulate prostitutes by dividing them into "classes," much as some European cities did (and still do). If a woman was found to suffer from venereal disease or other illness, she could be forced into a Social Evil Hospital until rendered "cured."

4

YOU CAN'T FIT A SQUARE PEG INTO A ROUND HOLE

LOVE IS A MANY-SPLINTERED THING

Ah love! The relations between a man and a woman can be tortured enough. But when you're not sure whether your role is

> *Remember, if you smoke after sex you're doing it too fast.*
>
> —ANONYMOUS

that of the male or female, it can get even dicier. Or if you happen to be both male AND female wrapped up in one. Or if you have no problem with your own gender, but the opposite one doesn't do it for you. These are the situations that can try (wo)men's souls. It's not as if gender confusion or same-sex partnerships are new issues, but they can make the already cloudy topic of sex even murkier.

WE'LL HAVE A GAY OLD TIME!

From Greek gods and heroes (such as Zeus and Hercules) to Roman emperor Nero, being gay was just dandy. In fact, the early Roman Empire recognized marriages between same-sex partners. Plato, da Vinci, and Michelangelo were all homosexuals who didn't hide their orientation.

In America during the 1800s, homosexuality, although not openly accepted, was neither illegal (as it would become) nor all that unusual. Lesbians would occasionally dress and live as

> *The good thing about masturbation is that you don't have to dress up for it.*
> —TRUMAN CAPOTE

men in order to earn men's wages and openly have relationships with other women, but two men or two women living together didn't garner much attention. Some gay men found gender-specific work camps or the male-intensive "wild West" the perfect foil for their lifestyle. Some historians steadfastly deny that many of these all-male arenas were hotbeds of homosexual activity, but the very fact that conservatives felt the need to rise up and create laws prohibiting "acts against nature" (at the time, a common euphemism for male-on-male anal or oral sex) implies otherwise.

In 1920 a survey of 1,200 single-female college graduates revealed that 28 percent of the women from exclusively female schools and 20 percent from coed schools admitted to carry-

> *I never miss a chance to have sex or appear on television.*
> —GORE VIDAL

ing on a homoerotic relationship at least once. But same-sex relations were coming under fire by the medical community and for the next half-century would be thought of as psychologically deviant.

WHY, OH WHY?

Numerous studies have tried to determine why some people prefer their own sex, but despite many theories there has been no evidence to suggest anything. Aristotle wrote in the fourth century B.C. that homosexuality was an inborn tendency likely to get stronger through habit. In the 1700s, French philosopher Voltaire believed it was a passing experience for everyone that normally goes away as a person matures into adulthood. Homosexuals, he believed, just don't progress as far.

In the late 1800s, a German named Richard von Krafft-Ebing proposed that homosexuality was hereditary. Of course, he didn't explain how they managed to proliferate, but there it is.

Freud, the famous observer of all that is penile, basically agreed with Voltaire—that humans are naturally bisexual prior to some point between puberty and adulthood.

Sex researcher Havelock Ellis wrote in the early 1900s that homosexuality was a natural, inborn predisposition that couldn't be changed.

Weak fathers, overbearing mothers, hormones, prenatal conditions, and sexual abuse have all been blamed for making a good guy go gay. But none of these speculations have ever been proven true.

So why are people gay? We dunno.

During World War II, gay men had plenty of opportunity to meet one another in the armed services. The intense same-sex environments provided plenty of time for relationships to develop. Gay women also had an easier time of it because

X-RATED MOVIE TITLES

The Bone Ranger
Bloobers and Boners
Position Impossible
Swallow My Pride
Sex a Foot
Assanova
No Silicone Zone

women were out in the working world and suddenly had far more mobility. In many cities, bars catering to gay clientele opened in the '40s. Once this subculture was formed, it took root and continued to grow, even after the war was over. But the male homosexual population was (and continues to be) much larger and more visible than its female counterpart. Is that because boys are more likely to prefer their own kind? Well, sociologists haven't really decided. The disparity may have more to do with women's ability to hide homosexual feelings from society (and even themselves), and the fact that they can perform heterosexually, regardless.

In the '50s, homophobia and paranoia reigned supreme. The slightest hint of "unmanliness" could be cause for suspicion. One theory contends that the fear of being labeled homosexual was one of the reasons for the relative stability of family during the era. Unmarried men, or those who abandoned their families, might be labeled queer. At the same time McCarthy was digging for commies, the Republicans (always a bit uptight) were freaking out about gays. Gay . . . oops that's Guy Gabrielson, the Republican National Chairman in 1950, said homo-

ANOTHER WAY TO SAY "FELLATIO"

Enjoying a tube steak

Talking with the bald man

Giving the soldier a good tongue lashing

Marinating the monkey

Wetting down the worm

Blowin' the love trumpet

Playing a tune on the fleshy flute

Puff the dragon

Whispering to willie

Giving Mr. Winky an oral report

Properly saluting the flagpole

Spit shining the weapon

sexuals were "perhaps as dangerous as actual communists." In June of that year, the Senate ordered a formal inquiry to unmask gays in the government. In 1953, Eisenhower barred homosexuals from the government payroll because gays were considered a security risk. The thinking was that homos were sexually indulgent and therefore weaker, thus being likely to spill government secrets to spies, or would be at risk for blackmail. This rationale led to police actions against gays, which in turn led to general actions against gays.

And then came the '60s. White college students, busy protesting the war, disdained traditional middle-class values and mainstream social conscience. Hippies were urging folks to

The turtle lives 'twixt plated decks which practically conceal its sex. I think it clever of the turtle in such a fix to be so fertile.

—ODGEN NASH

X-RATED MOVIE TITLES

Hooterville
Giant Cups, Gnarly Nipples
Motor Crotch
Gentlemen's Hind Quarters
Maiden Heaven
Nut Sucking Champions

"do their own thing." And the women's movement was questioning sex roles and the role of sex in society. The climate was ripe to inspire previously secret homosexuals to question the prejudices against them. The gay subculture started to rise to the surface as a political issue. Allen Ginsberg and his homoerotic *Howl* had won in court against obscenity charges, and the women's movement had taken lesbianism under its protective wing. (The women's movement actually ended up suffering drastically as a result, but it was a substantial contribution to gay rights.) In 1969, NYC police raided a gay bar in Greenwich Village called the Stonewall Inn. Patrons did not go quietly into the night. The resulting riot added fuel to the fire and less than a month later, the Gay Liberation Front was formed. Lesbians and gay men have continued to join together on political issues and have become strong enough that candidates regularly court them for support.

NINE OUT OF TEN AGREE, THE OTHER JUST WANTS TO GO HOMO

Alfred Kinsey shed some light on a subject previously kept in the dark. He reported 10 percent of white American males are homosexuals and that 37 percent had, at least once, a homosexual experience with another man that ended in orgasm.

He found only 3 percent of women admitted to being lesbians, with 19 percent having had some kind of lesbian experience.

While Kinsey's numbers are thought to still be valid for men today, it is generally believed that the numbers are way off for women, especially because bisexuality has become sort of hip on college campuses these days.

CAN I TRADE IN A FEW OF THESE PARTS?

Transsexuals are folks who feel they have somehow gotten the wrong sexual identity—guys who think they are really girls or girls who think they should have gotten a penis in their pants. This condition is not to be confused with your common household transvestite, who just gets a kick out of cross-dressing. Transsexuals have deep-seated gender identity issues, which go way beyond sexual desires. Lucky for them, there's hope. Way back in 1953, an American marine underwent an operation in Denmark in which doctors changed his physical appearance from male to female. She became instantly famous around the globe as Christine Jorgensen, the world's first sex-change recipient. Many have followed in his/her path. Experts estimate

ANOTHER WAY TO SAY "CUNNILINGUS"

Licking the cat
Muff diving
Carpet munching
Having a bite at beaver creek
Slurping the sideways smile
Canoe licking
Tuna snuffling
Having a boxed lunch at the Y
Licking the dew off her lily
Juicing the G-spot
Giving her a moustache ride
Wearing thighs on your ears
Whistling through the wheatfield

that 1 in 100,000 boys feel they should have been girls and that 1 in 130,000 girls want to be boys. Not all of them opt for "gender reassignment," but for those that do, how does that work?

Don't knock masturbation, it's sex with someone you love!
—WOODY ALLEN

First, regardless of whether a person is a male-to-female or female-to-male "tranny," they have to live openly as a person of the opposite sex for a year or two, during which they have many, many visits to old Dr. Psych's couch. They also start hormone therapy. Male-to-female transsexuals take daily doses of estrogen, which can promote breast growth, reduces erections, generally shrinks the interior male parts, and may raise the subject's voice pitch. Some male-to-female transsexuals have breast implants early on in the process, creating a sort of new breed of person—one who looks like a woman but has a functioning penis. Electrolysis is also helpful to remove un-wanted body and facial hair. Women choosing to become men take testosterone, which stops menstruation, deepens the voice, and promotes hair growth on the body and face. Finally, it's time for the surgery.

Changing a male into a female is the easier surgery. First the doctor removes the penis and testicles, then sculpts a vagina, complete with vulva and labia, out of the removed parts. Some transsexuals who have become women claim they can orgasm. To change a female into a male, first there is a complete hys-terectomy. Then the vagina is closed and the surrounding tissues removed. The doctor can then take skin from the abdomen, vaginal lips, and/or the perineum and fashion it into a penis. In these cases the penis only functions for urination, otherwise the damn thing is fairly useless. Although an implant to make it become erected can be added, some f-to-m transsexuals don't bother with the penis because it is such an extensive, expensive kind of surgery.

> *Is Sex Necessary?*
> —Title of book by James
> Thurber and E. B. White

In America the number of male-to-female and female-to-male surgeries are about equal. But overall, they've been re-duced because many of the hospitals and medical centers that used to do transsexual surgery no longer offer it. In part it is a question of money and insurance. But there has also been a question in the medical community in recent years as to whether the surgery is actually that beneficial to those that undergo it.

Oddly, transsexuals are not necessarily attracted to the op-

> **ANOTHER WAY TO SAY "INTERCOURSE"**
>
> Letting the eel swim upstream
> Sending the little sailor to sea
> Getting pounded with a love truncheon
> Getting some stinky on your hang-down
> Sinking in the pink
> Riding the baloney pony
> Giving her a little pickle tickle
> Skinny dipping in the love pond
> Sharpening the pencil

posite sex once they change. After sex reassignment surgery, the ratio of gay and straight transsexuals is roughly equal to the rest of the population.

WHO WEARS THE PANTIES IN THE FAMILY?

Transvestites are men who become sexually aroused by dressing in feminine clothing. They are usually straight and shouldn't be confused with drag queens. Drag queens are usually gay. The distinction is that drag queens enjoy the theatrics and drama of dressing as women, but don't depend on the clothing for arousal. Being a transvestite qualifies as a fetish and is usually not complicated by gender confusion or sexual preference.

Just to confuse things, however, there are now a number

Give me chastity and continence— but not yet.
—SAINT AUGUSTINE

ANOTHER WAY TO SAY "THE BOY IS MASTURBATING"

Burping the worm
Waxing the weezer
Wasting babies
Jackin' the beanstalk
Roughing up the suspect
Rubbing the magic lamp
Waxing the carrot
Cleaning the tube
Beef Strokin' off
Going blind
Kneading the noodle

of transvestites that have taken the surgical step of breast implants and masquerade as transsexual "chicks with dicks" for pornography. These guys often bill themselves as pre-op trannies, but they have no intention of actually becoming women.

THE MIGHTY HERMAPHRODITE

The word "hermaphrodite" refers to any organism that has sex organs of both male and female, such as many flowers. In humans, it means a genetic abnormality. There are three kinds of hermaphrodites: true, male pseudo, and female pseudo. Despite the way the category names sound, all three are equally hermaphroditic, if you will. Hermaphrodites may have female (XX) or male (XY) chromosomes, or a unique variety, such as XXY or XXYY. Physically, they may have a penis, one or two

ANOTHER WAY TO SAY "PENIS"

Wonder wand
Eleven inches of dangling death
Johnson
Boning tool
Bush blaster
Tallywacker
Joystick
The main vein
Mr. Happy

gonads, a vagina, vulva, etc. or any combination thereof. Unlike ancient myths, hermaphrodites cannot fuck themselves or procreate on their own. And unlike circus sideshow freaks, they are never, ever split vertically, male on one side, female on the other.

Is it not strange that desire should so many years outlive performance?
—SHAKESPEARE

The male pseudo has XY chromosomes and internal testes, but on the outside they usually have female genitalia or something sort of ambiguous. The female pseudo has XX chromosomes with a uterus and ovaries, but on the outside can actually have a penis.

For the pseudo hermaphrodites, it is a fairly simple error of mother nature. Surgery can correct the problem so the outside matches the inside. For the true hermaphrodite, however, doctors generally recommend assigning the sex most like the person's chromosome pattern and will do corrective surgery accordingly.

ANOTHER WAY TO SAY "VAGINA"
Fur burger
Camel toe
Willie's favorite parking space
Hothouse
Poon-tang
The hooded nub
Holiest of holies
Koochie
Love mussel
Pink snapper

In this politically correct age, hermaphrodites are also called androgynes or intersexes.

ALL BY MYSELF
or: "Don't touch that thing, you'll go blind!"

Some people just prefer their own company when it comes to having sex, and nowadays no one much cares. But masturbation has endured quite a bad reputation and has been blamed for blindness, insanity, epilepsy, acne, weight loss, decreased mental capacity, weakness, lethargy, and early death. Phew! It's a dangerous activity! Cures, aimed at parents for kids with curious hands, ranged from locks and cages to surgery. Some boys were made to wear metal mittens; others had their penises burnt. Extremists even had their children castrated. It wasn't unusual in the nineteenth century for parents to tie kids' hands to the bedposts at night. It seems the cures verged on being sickly sexual themselves. Gravies, oysters, spices, jellies, coffee, alcohol, and chocolate were all thought to increase the desire to masturbate.

Today, of course, experts agree that masturbation is a normal human activity, and some behaviorists recommend it to their patients.

5

YOU WANT TO DO *WHAT?*

Fetish is from the Latin for "really weird sex." Actually, it is "any object that causes a habitual erotic response." So whether it's

> *Existence permeates sexuality and vice versa. . .*
> —MAURICE MERLEAU-PONTY

big, white "Granny underwear," food, shoes, vampire fangs, latex rubber, whipped cream, hot candle wax, or a whip, if it consistently makes you hot, you're a fetishist.

Some fetishes make sense. Or, at least, from a psychological perspective, you can guess at their origins. If, as a young boy, your mother repeatedly spanked you with her shoe, and one time you became aroused, guess why you now go nuts over stiletto heels? The roots of other fetishes are more difficult to discern. Encasing yourself in latex rubber? To each his own. Let's look at some of the more unusual sexual practices around.

PORN-STAR NAMES
Alyssa Alps
Angel Hart
Asia Carrera
Barbara Dare
Busty Dusty

I'M JUST CARNAL ABOUT CARNYS

Most of us feel a curiosity when faced with physical oddities and deformities. In fact, the emotion is strong enough to have supported circus sideshows for decades. The "freak show" has lost a lot of its appeal in these more enlightened times, but people are generally fascinated, despite their repulsion or embarrassment, when faced with the unusual.

For a few folks, however, a deformity can bring unparalleled sexual arousal. Although not a common fetish, it has earned its own name—dysmorphophilia. (Some fetishes may be noted in medical or psychological journals but remain unnamed.)

Dismorphophics may be attracted to any number of disfigurements, including radical mastectomies. But if you've lost a limb, then an acrotomophiliast may be the mate for you. These characters are attracted to amputees. *Fascination* magazine caters to men with this particular fetish by featuring nothing but photos of female amputees. (One could also suppose *Fascination* might appeal to gay acrotomophiliasts, although there's probably not enough of them to improve the subscription numbers much.)

Good news for the fetishist whose kicks arise from eproctophilia! They certainly don't have to visit a circus or find some obscure

---

PORN-MOVIE TITLES

Three's Company
Aim to Thrill
All About Steve
Ass Attack
Backstage Sluts

---

literature to get their blood spinning. Despite the root word "procto," this obsession doesn't rely on a rectal exam or anal sex.

If you want to make an eproctophiliac happy, eat a nice dinner of beans, beans, beans and treat him (or her) to a veritable symphony of gaseous emissions. For it is both the sound and smell of farts—yup, farts—that brings ecstasy to these guys and gals.

TOP OR BOTTOM?

A form of sex play as opposed to a true fetish, domination and submission involve one person surrendering to another. A "bottom" is someone who agrees to be dominated. A "top" is the dominator. And, while some people pay to be dominated by professional dominatrixes, others engage in this kind of behavior within the realm of their primary relationship. Need a little discipline in your life?

Ways in which a top can "enforce" the rules and punish infractions during sessions include the following:

- dog collars
- diapers

PORN-MOVIE TITLES

Bad Ass Brunettes
Carnal Coeds
Forever Hung
Generation Sex
In Living Color
Mammary Lane

- whips
- slave collars
- bondage equipment
- costumes

Submissives find that being dominated relieves stress. Nothing like a spanking to take away your cares. Ouch! They may also feel as if allowing their partner to humiliate them to an extreme degree is a sign of love. Diamonds used to be forever. Now it's that divine little dog collar. People who feel guilty about having sex also may like the submissive role because it takes away a level of personal responsibility.

"Slaves" often bond with one "master" or "mistress." In this case, they may totally care for their master's personal needs including giving him or her a bath, shaving them, brushing hair, applying nail polish—and even doing housework. Clean that oven . . . scrub the floors . . . then hold your mistress's vibrator. Very often slaves will indicate their devotion by body-part worship, with the most common part worshiped being the feet. Which brings us to:

PORN-STAR NAMES
Celeste
Chasey Lain
Chloe Jones
Crystal Wilder
Danyel Cheeks
Devin Deray
Drew Berrymore

I'M JUST A LITTLE MORE FOCUSED
THAN THE AVERAGE GUY!

Certain body parts have awesome powers of attraction. Some men will even claim their favorites—as in, "I'm a breast man" or "leg man." And many women will admit to being enticed by a fine specimen of their preferred body part such as a hairy chest, a firm behind, or big, honkin' biceps.

There is a point, however, where passion for a particular part crosses over into the realm of the fetish. From eyeballs to toes, there are folks out there who are hot for a special spot. Pygophilia refers to those who find ecstasy in kissing buttocks. (We've all known a boss or two who wanted one of THESE guys.) Of course, everyone's heard of one. . . .

In the Feet of the Night

Plug in "foot fetish" on any Internet search engine and be prepared to find hundred of sites dedicated to this practice.

WHAT'S YOUR PORN NAME? PART I

You, too, can be a porn star. That's right, According to this game,

1. Take your first pet's name.
2. Add your mother's maiden name.

Voilà! Porn star du jour!
Does it work?
Erica Orloff's porn name? . . . Buttons Cunningham
Sad but true.

There are "gas pedal girls"—up-close photos of women's bare feet pressed to the gas pedal, as well as many barefoot models. Only most of them probably don't realize they are the darlings of the Net. Christie Brinkley, America's golden-haired sweetheart, recently posed for a women's magazine with her daughter Sailor. Christie donned a pair of jeans for the shoot, but she didn't wear shoes. Some creative foot lover then took her magazine photo and blew up Christie's toes, pedicured and all, for the many fetishists out there.

High heels also appeal to foot fetishists—some men even like their penises massaged by a woman's stiletto. Other fetishists like the smell and submissive nature of kissing feet as well as worshiping the feet of their mistresses. Smelly feet? Okay, you may say, but at least it's not body odor. But wait . . .

PORN STAR NAMES
Ginger Lynn
Heather Hunter
Holly Body
Houston
Hyapatia Lee

Armpit Goddesses

Armpit lovers of America, unite. There is a web site for you. "Some smell 'em, some lick 'em," say these armpit lovers . . . but "we love 'em." Yes . . . armpits. Clean shaven and sexy. Once again, many models and actresses have no idea their pits are the envy of fetishists. But these fetishists take magazine photos of models in which their arms are raised over their heads. Download your favorite supermodel's pit today—up close and blown up one hundred times.

In Europe, where women often grow their armpit hair, it is not uncommon for those who like armpits (axillists) to rub a penis in the woman's armpit hair and build friction this way.

INFANTILISM

Need a little TLC? A little babying? A *lot* of babying? Then maybe infantilism is for you. For many who practice this, infantilism is an escape from the cares and worries of the grown-up world. Some people escape to Club Med. Infantilists escape by acting like a big baby. They may enjoy the following practices:

> ## WHAT'S YOUR PORN NAME? PART II
>
> Okay, so Buttons Cunningham isn't sending men in droves to the video store. So here's another technique for deriving your porn star name.
>
> 1. Take your middle name.
> 2. Add your street name.
>
> Voilà! You're a porn star. Or are you?
> Erica Orloff's porn-star name using this method? Joan Tranquilla.
> Slightly better than Buttons Cunningham, but no "Christy Canyon."

- breast sucking
- enemas
- toilet training
- diapers
- rubber pants

They may also pay a professional dominatrix or "Mommy" to discipline them, change their diapers, powder their (big) bottoms, and offer them pacifiers. Waaaaaaaaa! There are even adult baby clubs where multiple "babies" can enjoy a large playpen. Isn't little Junior just adorable?

LET'S HAVE A LOOK AT THAT

And then there are those for whom the eyes do it.

You might think a person who likes to watch and one who likes to be looked at would be perfectly suited to one another, but it ain't always true. While there are happy couples in which one party actually has sex (with themselves or others), while the other gets their jollies by observing, the looker and the lookee are not always on the same page.

For the cliché exhibitionist with his obligatory trenchcoat, the excitement of exhibiting himself is inextricably tied to the viewer's dismay at being presented with such a naughty sight. Conversely, the peeper often gets as much satisfaction from the viewee's ignorance of the peeping as from the actual sighting. Peeping is actually quite popular (not everyone who owns a telescope is really into amateur astronomy, you know), and often doesn't qualify as a fetish.

But some have honed their preferences to a fine point, and if their practices can't be characterized as fetishes, they certainly are unusual. One example is tithioscopia, which is a long word that means getting horny at the sight of a baby nursing at its mother's breast. (Paging Dr. Freud . . .)

Another curious habit for the looker/lookee set is called dogging. No, it doesn't mean letting your dog watch your sexual activities. It's a slang term for the practice of a couple having intercourse in a car while others stand around looking in the windows. Sounds like the perfect diversion if you find yourself at a bad movie at the drive-in!

Perhaps going back to that age-old mothers' admonishment "You can look but you can't touch," folks have been makin' money off the desire to sneak a peek. The Japanese, however, have put an interesting twist on this old turn-on—coffee houses that offer a spice a tad more exotic than Madagascar cinnamon. They have mirrored floors so that patrons can get a glimpse of what's up their server's skirt.

POP QUIZ

QUESTIONS *(Answers start on page 107.)*

1. What is sexual ecouteurism?
   A. being aroused by wearing the undergarments of the opposite sex
   B. being aroused by hearing someone else having sex
   C. being aroused by watching jungle animals (as opposed to domesticated pets) having sex
   D. being aroused by watching female wrestlers or boxers

2. Old Maid's Insanity is slang for?
   A. transvestites who like to dress like spinsters from the 1940s
   B. transvestites who act out vignettes and pretend to be "old maids"
   C. people who believe someone who barely knows them is secretly in love with them
   D. a card game played by S&M participants in which different cards represent specific punishments

3. What, according to the Kinseys, is the percentage of men who can perform autofellatio (performing fellatio on themselves)?
   A. approximately 2 percent
   B. approximately .002 percent
   C. zero (They guess the number to be statistically insignificant.)
   D. approximately 5 to 7 percent

4. In a certain harem, with over 600 women in it, what did the sultan allow?
   A. lesbianism (There was no way he could satisfy all the women.)
   B. dildos (There was no way he could satisfy all the women—and this way they could satisfy themselves.)
   C. group sex (There was no way he could satisfy all the women, so he allowed, one night a week, men in his command to come to the harem and have anonymous sex with the women who had to leave veils over their faces.)
   D. erotic movies to be made (Some of the earliest erotic films were made of this harem, and the women in them were considered exotic and exceedingly beautiful. Silent films, with only three or four remaining in circulation among private collectors, they are now worth in the hundreds of thousands of dollars.)

5. Who was St. Pazzi?
   A. a famous hot wax enthusiast
   B. a famous prostitute known for her fellatio skills in the Roaring Twenties

C. a famous stripper with enormous, real (pre-implant invention) breasts

D. a famous transvestite who could sing like Ethel Merman

6. What does hybristophilia have to do with Charles Manson?
   A. Hybristophiliasts fall in love with people who have committed crimes or are in prison.
   B. He enjoyed group sex.
   C. His groupies or family members were aroused by self-mutilation in the form of "jailhouse" tattoos.
   D. He was a secret homophobe.

7. What is Slippery Stuff?
   A. a massage oil
   B. a sexual lubricant
   C. the code word for semen used in Monica Lewinsky's diary
   D. an herb concoction, containing the ingredient slippery elm, sold through mail-order catalogs that supposedly allows men to stay erect for up to 90 minutes—a sort of natural "Viagra"

8. What is a Burmese ball?
   A. a ball held during the period after Lent, in which group sex is often held with people wearing elaborate masks to hide their identity
   B. a ball held by members of the Burmese Boinking Society of San Francisco during which massive mud pits are assembled and gay men hold mud wrestling championships

C. a ball of hard cheese with a pungent smell used to punish during S&M sessions

D. a ball inserted into the penis

9. What is a medocure?

A. a person who is aroused by medical personnel

B. a person who is aroused by taking foul-tasting medicine (Originating in childhood, medocures often create disgusting homemade "medicine" or potions and have their partners administer it.)

C. dressing up male genitalia with glitter

D. a female impersonator who dresses as a nurse

10. What is *Venus in Furs?*

A. an X-rated movie depicting transexuals having sex on fur coats

B. a book about domination by beautiful women

C. a famous sculpture that angered the U.S. Senate when it was discovered that money for the arts had been used to give a grant to a sculptor who depicted an outrageously sexual woman with enormous breasts, a protruding tongue, a dildo around her neck, and fake pubic hair completely covering the sculpture's marble body

D. a porn movie showing naked women in fur coats— and that's it—for a special type of fetishist aroused by fur

11. What is satyriasis?

A. the male equivalent of nymphomania

B. a sexually transmitted disease, long since eradicated by the invention of antibiotics

C. the term for sexual relations with a sheep or goat

D. named for a Greek god of food, it is sexual arousal through the use of food or drink

12. If you ran into the Lesbian Sex Mafia, who would you be hangin' with?

A. a group of lesbians who run a gambling syndicate outside Chicago

B. a group of lesbians who engage in elaborate Godfather movie reenactments culminating in group sex

C. an S&M support group for lesbians

D. a group of lesbians who traditionally march in Gay Pride parades dressed as 1940s-era gangsters

13. What is botulinonia?

A. self-scarring or mutilation

B. sexual relations with a sausage

C. sexual arousal related to vomiting

D. sexual arousal related to school fantasies such as being spanked by a headmistress, Catholic girls' school uniforms, etc.

ANSWERS

1. B. being aroused by hearing someone else having sex

2. C. people who believe someone who barely knows them is secretly in love with them

3. B. approximately .002 percent (In order to do this, a man must have an unusually long penis, coupled with being extraordinarily limber.)

4. B. dildos (There was no way he could satisfy all the women—and this way they could satisfy themselves.)

5. A. a famous hot wax enthusiast (Not only was this person a hot wax enthusiast, she was a nun who used hot wax to prove her piety, having it dripped on her while she was tied down.)

6. A. (Hybristophiliasts fall in love with people who have committed crimes or are in prison. His "family" is an example of such a phenomena.)

7. B. a sexual lubricant (It was originally designed to help divers get into their wet suits, but people have found it makes an excellent sexual lubricant.)

8. D. a ball inserted into the penis (Supposedly, these balls, inserted under the skin and then held in place with stitches or bandages until healing occurs, make the penis larger and increase sexual pleasure.)

9. C. dressing up male genitalia with glitter (Or dying male pubic hair, dressing up a penis with stickers or body paint—in general it is adorning and beautifying the male genitalia region.)

10. B. a book about domination by beautiful women (A novelist of the 1800s wrote sexual fantasies about beautiful women humiliating and disciplining men.)

11. A. the male equivalent of nymphomania

12. C. an S&M support group for lesbians

13. B. sexual relations with a sausage

6

SEXSTYLES OF
THE RICH AND FAMOUS

Of the delights of this world, man cares most for sexual intercourse, yet he has left it out of his heaven.
—MARK TWAIN

Did we *really* have to know what President Clinton did with his cigar? In this day and age, the *whiff* of sex brings endless media speculation. If it isn't being reported in magazines and newspapers, then it's being confessed to Barbara Walters on television. But the public is also part of the equation. Face it, you bought this book. We love to know what the rich and famous are doing behind closed bedroom doors. Americans love gossip, gossip, gossip. So come on . . . did you hear about . . . ?

PORN-MOVIE TITLES
O-Zone
Natural Knockers
Out and About
Rear View Mirror
North Pole
Dougie Hoser, M.D.

THE GROPE THAT *NEVER* WAS

One of the best Old Hollywood stories of sex and scandal is actually a story of sex that never was. Hedda Hopper and Louella Parsons were the vicious purveyors of gossip in the early days of Hollywood. They wielded the power to ruin a reputation or whole lives with their columns . . . and neither one seemed to much care if what she printed was true or not.

In the face of lies and humiliation, most stars just tried to ignore the gossip—and many an up-and-comer found they could never find real work in Hollywood again. Clara Bow was one woman ruined by lies and innuendo. But her story later. First, the grope that never was.

Maureen O'Hara, the beautiful, flame-haired actress of such classics as *The Quiet Man* and *How Green Was My Valley,* was alleged in a gossip column to have openly engaged in indecent behavior in the balcony of a movie theater. Her breasts were (shock!) groped and she had a major make-out session and *more, dear readers,* with (gasp, horrors) a young Latin lover. People were scandalized that a star of such stature would lower herself to such a public display of indiscretion. Only problem with this gossip item was that it was all a bold lie. But instead of keeping quiet, O'Hara, noted for her iron will, decided to fight back.

> *Copulation was, I'm sure, Marilyn's uncomplicated way of saying "Thank you."*
> —NUNNALLY JOHNSON, director

Maureen O'Hara sued against the gossips and won. She proved in open court that she was overseas when the entire incident supposedly took place. A passport easily settled the matter. The columnists were shown to be liars and flagrant inventors of rumors, and this was the beginning of the end of their power in Hollywood.

It was the breast grope felt 'round the world. Or rather . . . not felt.

PACK OF TROJANS, ANYONE?

> *Looked like she was a cold dish with a man until you got her pants down, then she'd explode.*
> —GARY COOPER, on Princess Grace of Monaco (when she was merely Grace Kelly)

Clara Bow, of old-time Hollywood, was the center of a swirling storm of gossip. First she was named as the "other woman" in a nasty divorce scandal (in which Clara had to pay the betrayed wife for alienation of affection). Then her personal secretary sold scandalous tales of Clara's prolific love life to a sleazy tabloid. While some of the affairs were probably true—including Bela Lugosi, Eddie Cantor, Frederic March, and Gary Cooper—when Clara tried to fight back against her secretary, the gossip took a decidedly ugly turn.

According to the tabloid, egged on by Clara's now-fired personal secretary, Clara loved to entertain Trojans in her

PORN-STAR NAMES

Jasmone St. Clair
Jenna Jameson
Juli Ashton
Julie Strain (Judge Julie from Playboy's "Sex Court")
Kobe Tai
Kylie Ireland

home—the University of Southern California's Trojans, that is. Gangbangs, beer parties, and naked football . . . it was all so much tabloid-newspaper ink. She supposedly frequented the Trojans' frat houses, provided them with bootleg alcohol, and showered them with gifts. The then-unknown John Wayne (Marion Morrison) allegedly bedded Clara, along with all the line-backers, defensive backs, and anyone in football pads. So, was Clara a Trojan-lover? Yes . . . she loved the sports team, and she liked a good time, including poker games, gambling, and parties. But it appears her secretary wanted revenge, and much of Clara's exploits were exploitative lies. Still, Clara ended up fading out of Hollywood, and she suffered a number of nervous breakdowns to boot.

YOUNG AND RESTLESS

Other early Hollywood sex scandals centered around Charlie Chaplin, who had an affinity for young women. When he was 35, he married his 16-year-old girlfriend, who was already pregnant . . . though Charlie had first met her when she was a

7- or 8-year-old schoolgirl. For years, Charlie had been known for his affinity for young girls. But he wasn't the only one who ever indulged in underage *amours*.

Errol Flynn, Roman Polanski, Elvis Presley, Rob Lowe . . . all were alleged to enjoy women young enough to make their encounters illegal. Polanski eventually fled the United States after being caught in the middle of a statutory rape case.

> *I don't wear panties anymore—this startles the Hollywood wolves so much they don't know what to pull at, so they leave me alone.*
> —MAMIE VAN DOREN (long before Sharon Stone)

Alleged . . . alleged . . . how do the gossips get away with all these innuendoes and stories, particularly if they can't prove them?

ARE YOU BLIND?

Welcome to the blind item.

"What Hollywood superstar recently bedded his sexy co-star while his pregnant wife was home pining away for her husband?"

> *Shall we shag now or shall we shag later?*
> —AUSTIN POWERS

"What Hollywood super couple is known for their intense lovemaking sessions. They are so intense, in fact, that they have a private doctor who sets their broken bones and tends to their bruises with utmost secrecy. However, friends of these well-known lovebirds are afraid the couple is actually getting out of control."

PORN-MOVIE TITLES
Edward Penishands
Heidi's House
Hillbilly Honeys
Big Babes in Budapest
Day of Decadence
Copz in the Hood

The blind item is a brief paragraph that insinuates someone in Hollywood is doing the nasty with someone they're not supposed to be doing it with . . . or has a kinky side they don't want made public. Are these blind items true? Sometimes. What goes on behind closed doors can't usually be proved, but Hollywood stars have extensive staffs and, well, walls can sometimes be thin. And tabloids are known to pay cash for good "dish."

"What *Dirty Little Secrets* author once had a lost weekend in the 1980s, during which . . ."

Oops!

ISN'T THAT AGAINST THE TEN COMMANDMENTS?

Of course, Hollywood isn't the only town with sex scandals, and actors and actresses don't have the corner market on racy tales. Religious figures have been caught in some pretty outrageous situations.

Pope John XII was beaten to death by the betrayed husband of one of his mistresses. In fact, he had so many mistresses that

PORN-STAR NAMES

Letha Weapons
Lisa Lipps
Marilyn Chambers
Mimi Miyagi
Nici Sterling
Nikki Dial
Nikki Tyler

they say the papal palace resembled a brothel. (Perhaps we should have put him in the "Can't Buy Me Love chapter.")

Pope Alexander VI went beyond having mistresses to fathering children out-of-wedlock—at least seven according to historians. And apparently his virility didn't wane with age. In his 60s, he had a 16-year-old girlfriend. The Holy See was apparently seeing more than he was supposed to.

> *All discarded lovers should be given a second chance, but with somebody else.*
> —MAE WEST

RAGGED DICK

Horatio Alger wrote many novels about rags-to-riches American ingenuity. He was one of the most successful American authors of his generation (mid-to-late 1800s) His books often followed the exploits of young boys such as Ragged Dick and Phil the Fiddler. These young men, through their hard work ethic, rose above their poor circumstances to enjoy success.

PORN-MOVIE TITLES

Eight is Never Enough
Fetish Therapy
My Baby Got Back
Nympho Bride
Nici Nici Gang Bang
The Assman
A Passage Through India
Anal Cannibals

This kind of "pull yourself up by the boot-straps" mentality was just what Americans needed to hear. Of course, Horatio Alger had some skeletons in his closet that America didn't need to hear about. It appears that Horatio, a clergyman and minister in Massachusetts, particularly took an interest in the young boys in his parish. The girls could apparently burn in hell for all Horatio cared. In fact, his behavior was considered somewhat disturbing and a full investigation was launched, during which Horatio confessed to homosexual activities with the sons of a couple of his parishioners. So ended a promising ministerial career. Horatio Alger became a writer. And just think, if he hadn't been caught, we wouldn't have Ragged Dick. Or a fiddling Phil.

PORN-MOVIE TITLES

Anus and Andy
Booty Double
Butt Masters
Boys Night Out
Luciano's Lucky Ladies
Saleswoman in Heat
Salt and Pepper Boys
A Cockwork Orange
Alice in Hollyweird

NEVER MARRY A NYMPHOMANIAC

> *I love Mickey Mouse more than any woman I have ever known.*
> —WALT DISNEY (1901–1966)

While marrying a nymphomaniac might be a male fantasy . . . if you were a homosexual man in a sham marriage with a nymphomaniac woman, it could be a recipe for disaster. But that's precisely what genius composer Pyotr Ilich Tchaikovsky did. Tchaikovsky, a self-hating homosexual, married one of his pupils. The unstable young woman, Antonina Ivanova Miliukova, was unconvinced by family and friends that marrying a man with an affinity for male lovers would not be a wise choice. The marriage was doomed from the start.

> *My advice to you is get married: if you find a good wife you'll be happy; if not, you'll become a philosopher.*
> —SOCRATES (470–399 B.C.)

Tchaikovsky, unable to consummate the marriage, and certainly unable to fulfill the nympho's needs, tried to commit suicide by standing in an

SIX DEGREES OF SEXUAL SEPARATION

In the age of AIDS, doctors and health-care officials say that you aren't just having sex with the person you're sleeping with, but with every person *that* person has ever had sex with. This leads to some pretty exponential numbers. It also leads to some pretty weird sex partners.

For starters, Al Pacino bedded Frank Sinatra . . . a couple of times removed.
Frank Sinatra was married to Mia Farrow.
Mia Farrow's long-term partner was Woody Allen.
Woody Allen's long-term partner was Diane Keaton.
Diane Keaton's long-term partner was Al Pacino.

Carmen Electra and Joan Collins?
Joan Collins had an affair with Warren Beatty.
Warren Beatty had an affair with Madonna.
Madonna romped with Dennis Rodman.
Dennis Rodman was married to Carmen Electra.

Play the fame game for yourself!

icy river. Though he did not die, he left his wife . . . and shortly thereafter lapsed into a coma from his icy-river fiasco. Though he recovered, Tchaikovsky later drank unboiled water during an epidemic and died. Some scholars say it was stupidity; others claim it was suicide.

And what became of his nymphomaniac wife? Like a true nymphomaniac, she took many lovers and tirelessly had sex

PORN-MOVIE TITLES

Dirty Bob's Xcellent Adventures
Hell on Heels
Philmore Butts: Taking Care of Business
America's Nastiest Home Videos
Bad Medicine
Best of Footworship

with them, bore illegitimate children, and eventually died in an insane asylum.

SICK IN EVERY WAY

Adolf Hitler, one of the most hated men in history, was rumored to have a very strange and sordid sex life—one that drove at least one lover to suicide.

Hitler took one of his young nieces as a lover when he was in his late thirties. Geli, the young daughter of his half-sister, was originally excited by the attentions of the fast-becoming powerful man. They were surrounded by bodyguards, assistants, a chauffeur, and the trappings of success, eventually moving to a fancy apartment in Munich. While at first his attentions and the attention the two of them drew when they were out together were headily intoxicating to the girl, she soon found his crazed possessiveness stifling. Everywhere Geli went, two Nazi chaperons accompanied her. She couldn't do anything without her uncle's permission.

Speculation on Hitler's sex life has swirled around for de-

ISN'T THAT ROMANTIC?

Hordes of women have discovered there's nothing like a little soft porn to spice up an ordinary day.

Mass produced, cheap paperback romances produced by companies such as Harlequin and Silhouette sell by the millions. Most follow a simple formula plot punctuated by detailed descriptions of sexual activity. Rarely direct, these descriptions use metaphors and euphemisms galore and range from the ridiculous to the sublime. Occasionally, they sound downright dangerous or painful, what with all the plundering and inflaming. Here are a few samples of this lusty literature.

"She felt her body opening to an alien fullness."

". . . he gently probed the dark sweet mystery of her."

"He felt awed by the profundity of their lovemaking."

"It was a long, wet, eating kiss."

"His manhood quivered beneath her brazen touch."

"He sipped her sweetness."

cades. Though definitive proof is not available, it is alleged that Geli and Hitler were involved in a relationship with dark psychological undertones (Shocking? It's hardly as if Hitler's known for his bon vivant gaiety). She apparently implied to others that their relations were "unnatural," and it is further alleged that he enjoyed being humiliated in the bedroom and watching her urinate, as well as other up-close and personal acts.

Despairing, Geli shot herself after Hitler refused to allow her to travel to Vienna on holiday while he was away. Thereafter,

PORN-MOVIE TITLES

Bums Away
Cherry Cheerleaders
Gazongas
Hole in One
House of Sleeping Beauties
Hurts So Good

Hitler plunged into a deep depression and shunned meat. (Dr. Freud? House call please.)

URBAN LEGENDS

Okay, no book about Dirty Little Secrets would be complete without exploring some of those secrets that keep getting repeated year after year. We're talking celebrity and famous person bullshit stories. So here are the most notorious:

- Richard Gere had to have a gerbil removed from his butt.
- Rod Stewart had to have semen pumped from his stomach.
- Elton John had to have semen pumped from his stomach.
- _____ (fill in rock star of the moment) had to have semen pumped from his stomach.
- Catherine the Great died from trying to screw a well-endowed horse.
- Neil Armstrong tried to get his neighbor some oral sex by saying his name over his moon transmission: "Good Luck, Mr. Gorky." (Legend has it Mr. Gorky's wife said she

would next give her husband oral sex when "the kid" next door walks on the moon.)

Well folks, though these are all good stories, they're also all false. No semen. No gerbils. No oral sex from the moon.

PROLIFIC FUCKERS

Okay, so some of us are getting more than our fair share of banging. The lists below are of famous persons and their equally famous alleged sexual partners. These are the men and women who are wearing out mattresses.

BANGER: Mick Jagger
ALLEGED BANGS: David Bowie, Carla Bruni, Jerry Hall, Bianca Jagger, Pamela Des Barres, Marianne Faithful, Margaret Trudeau, Carly Simon, MacKenzie Phillips, Linda Ronstadt

BANGER: Warren Beatty
ALLEGED BANGS: Brigitte Bardot, Isabelle Adjani, Joan Collins, Vivian Leigh, Michelle Phillips, Diane Sawyer, Carly Simon, Natalie Wood, Mamie Van Doren

BANGER: John F. Kennedy
ALLEGED BANGS: Joan Crawford, Jacqueline Kennedy Bouvier Onassis, Angie Dickinson, Marilyn Monroe, Gene Tierney, Lee Remick, Zsa Zsa Gabor

BANGER: Liza Minnelli
ALLEGED BANGS: Adam Ant, Edward Albert, Jr., Desi Arnaz,

Jr., Jack Haley, Jr., Mikhail Baryshnikov, Ryan O'Neal, Ben Vereen, Gene Simmons

BANGER: Jack Nicholson
ALLEGED BANGS: Candice Bergen, Faye Dunaway, Anjelica Huston, Meryl Streep, Margaret Trudeau, Rebecca Broussard, Michelle Phillips

BANGER: Mamie Van Doren
ALLEGED BANGS: Warren Beatty, Tony Curtis, Johnny Carson, Jack Dempsey, Eddie Fisher, Rock Hudson, Elvis Presley, Burt Reynolds

BANGER: Natalie Wood
ALLEGED BANGS: Warren Beatty, Raymond Burr, James Dean, Nicky Hilton, Jr., Dennis Hopper, Tab Hunter, Robert Wagner, Elvis Presley, Frank Sinatra, Christopher Walken

BANGER: Frank Sinatra
ALLEGED BANGS: Lauren Bacall, Jacqueline Bisset, Marlene Dietrich, Ava Gardner, Patty Duke, Mia Farrow, Zsa Zsa Gabor, Grace Kelly, Nancy Reagan, Marilyn Monroe, Gloria Vanderbilt, Natalie Wood

BANGER: Marlon Brando
ALLEGED BANGS: Ursula Andress, Tallulah Bankhead, Brigitte Bardot, Faye Dunaway, Joan Collins, Rita Moreno, Shelly Winters

BANGER: Mae West
ALLEGED BANGS: Bugsy Siegel, Anthony Quinn, George Raft,

David Niven, Joe Lewis, Harry Houdini, Cary Grant, Gary Cooper, Jack Dempsey

BANGER Cary Grant
ALLEGED BANGS: Dyan Cannon, Joan Crawford, Doris Duke, Howard Hughes.

7

IS IT OR ISN'T IT?

> The difference between pornography
> and erotica is lighting
>
> —GLORIA LEONARD

No book on dirty little secrets would be complete without a discussion of "bangless" sex. We're talking about the Internet.

When the scientists, government workers, and computer geeks who invented the Internet created this medium, they never would have guessed that porn and Internet relationships would take over cyberspace. Sure, they were thinking this was a way to transfer data over a computer. But then along came . . .

PORN-MOVIE TITLES
Kinky Nurses
Love Seats
Made in Heaven
Not with My Wife
Skippy, Jif and Jam

THE BANGLESS BANG

So, is it or isn't it? If your significant other is spending significant time as Busty Babs in the "Married and Looking" chat room, and she meets HungHarry and they "chat" about what they'd like to do to each other, are Babs and Harry cheating? If you catch your hubby typing down-and-dirty spanking fantasies to a cyber dominatrix, is he a dirty dog? (Or does he just want Mistress to treat him like one?)

Is the bangless bang cheating or harmless fantasy?

And who would have guessed twenty years ago that we'd be dealing with this question?

BABS OR HARRY?

Whether you think the zipperless cyberfuck is cheating or not kind of depends on whether or not you're Babs or Harry.

Men are my hobby, if I ever got married I'd have to give it up.
—MAE WEST

Many men see the Internet as a harmless diversion, while women are more likely to see a cyber affair as a betrayal.

> *Is it not true that sex degrades woman . . . if it is any good.*
> —ALAN PARTRIDGE,
> BBC Radio 4

Is it?

In cyber relationships, feelings can be very real. People have left their wives and husbands over on-line affairs. Then again, to others, it's a diversion like *Playboy* magazine or a little harmless flirting at the company Christmas party.

Let's ask Bill Clinton. If he can define receiving a blow job up close and personal from Monica as outside his "definition" of sex, then it's easy to see why countless computer clickers think getting their kicks in the "Hottub" chat room is innocent fun.

CHAT ABOUT THAT

Internet chat involves adopting "a handle" or cyber nickname and entering a "room" where you can "talk" in real time to other people about a variety of subjects. While you can find chat rooms on everything from stamp collecting to poetry to news events, you can also find plenty of chat rooms dedicated to those of us out there lookin' for love on the Net. Here's a glimpse at some of the Internet chat rooms devoted to cyber flirting:

- flirt.com
- netflirt.com
- meetmeonline.com
- singlesstop.com
- americansingles.com
- chatropolis.com

In these various cyber communities, are "rooms." If you
think of it as a hierarchy, the top
level is the bigger web commu-

> *Is that a gun in your pocket, or are
> you just glad to see me?*
>
> —MAE WEST

nity as a whole, and then a place like flirt.com is a smaller community of people looking for a relationship. Smaller, too, is a
specific "room" where real-time chats can occur. They can occur in rooms such as

- married and looking
- married and he's outta town
- goddesses
- hot tubs
- cyber pubs

AND YOU CHOSE THAT NAME?

Okay. So you've decided you want to see what all this cyber
sex is about. Now you have to join a chat group and choose
a handle. A recent spin through several chat rooms offered up
these names:

MALE NAMES:
Hotrod
Shambles
MangoMan
Highway Child
WillyBoy (See! Bill Clinton DOES approve of chat
    rooms!)
IrreverentJoe

PORN-STAR NAMES
Pandora Peaks
Paula Price
Porsche Lynn
Porn Queens
P. J. Sparxx
Rebecca Wild
Rocki Roads
Sandra Scream

Cashman
RacoonMan

FEMALE NAMES:
WildChild
Honey
Candy
Christy
Monica (See Willy Boy above)
HotStuff
KissMe

WALK THE WALK OR TALK THE TALK

Once online and surfing for love in all the wrong places, there are still two options. You can surf personal ads (one site boasts over one million personals) for people you might actually want to meet someday in much the same way that people answer

PORN-MOVIE TITLES

Smarty Pants
Bimbo Cheerleaders from Outer Space
Caught from Behind
Dirty Dr. Feelgood
Full Metal Bikini
Army Brat

classified personal ads from the newspaper. You can then e-mail them and strike up a cyber relationship first, which can then perhaps lead to a meeting in the real world.

The other option is simply to talk the talk. You can remain an anonymous chatter or even a "lurker" (someone who enters chat rooms but does not participate). Cyber flirting is enough for people like this . . . which leads us to . . .

MY NAME IS HARRY, AND I AM REALLY A HAIRY-BACKED GORILLA

Because people can adopt "handles," the Internet is one way to have truly anonymous, zipperless sex. Many people adopt alter egos so they can indulge another side of themselves, even changing genders. Other times, married people or people in relationships will use the chat rooms as a way of flirting and having cybersex without actually going out and cheating in that ol' biblical sense (because the Bible never did address virtual reality).

> *Some people grin and bear it; others smile and do it.*
>
> —ANONYMOUS

PORN-MOVIE TITLES

Barbara the Barbarian
Beauty and the Beast
Bed Over Babes
Best of Anal Annie
Between a Rock and a Hot Place
Black Bimbos in Heat
Call Girl Academy
Cat on a Hot Sin Roof

So, you may think you are talking to HungHarry, a tall, handsome, well-endowed lawyer who makes two million dollars a year and has the stamina of an 18-year-old stud boy, but Harry may really be a five-foot two-inch nebbish with glasses and a case of eczema. BustyBabs? She may be someone's Grandma.

WANNA PLAY?

So let's hop in a hot tub and see what happens in the world of chat. The following is a compilation of comments taken from various chat rooms and modified for privacy:

FEMALE CHATTER: OOOOOOOOOOHHHH . . . giggle . . .
   that water feels so good on my back.
MALE CHATTER: Tough day?
FEMALE CHATTER: Very. I need a full-body massage. Any
   takers?

PORN-MOVIE TITLES

City Lickers
Flesh for Frankenstein
Getting Off on Broadway
Hitler Sucks
Hometown Hookers
I Cream of Genie
Mad About You
Motel Sweets
She's America's Most Wanted
Sinset Blvd.

MALE CHATTER NUMBER 2: {{{{{{{}}}}}}}}}}}} [symbol for a big hug] Come over here. I'll rub you where it hurts.

FEMALE CHATTER: That feels great. Why don't you rub me down here, too.

MALE CHATTER: I'll take the front.

MALE CHATTER NUMBER 2: I'll rub her from behind on her nice firm ass. Very nice, (female's nickname).

FEMALE CHATTER: If I bend over, can you rub me some more? I really need some stress relief, if you know what I mean.

MALE CHATTER 2: How about if I rub my cock here?

FEMALE CHATTER: Now we're talking.

Yes . . . indeed we are. So, if you talk the talk, is it a cheat? And how did chat and cybersex become such a phenomena? The Net is very egalitarian. It doesn't much matter your race,

When I'm good I'm very, very good, but when I'm bad, I'm better.
—MAE WEST

MORE ROMANCE 'TWEEN THE PAGES

". . . [He] gently stroked the moist heat of her womanhood."

"She vanished into a vast, impenetrable cloud of love."

"Pastel ribons were untied . . . a zipper was lowered and left gaping open."

"He hypnotized her with forbidden love."

". . . he fit her exactly to the hard thrust of him. And she nearly lost consciousness at the stabbing ache of pleasure . . ."

He "spent an inordinately long time examining her breasts with his tongue."

"He slipped his finger into the sweet center of her."

". . . a dark and fierce emanation [came] from him."

". . . he spilled the essence of his strength into her and she exalted in receiving it because there was no taking it back."

". . . their tongues tangled tempestuously."

". . . he unwrapped her like an early Christmas present."

". . . one pink and white breast saucily uncovered"

"His arm curved around the small of her back, bending her like a blade of grass."

". . . thrust himself into her moist sheath."

religion, what kind of car you drive, how much is in your bank account, how tall you are, or how much you weigh. It doesn't matter if the closest you can get to touching your toes is your knees, your receding hairline is a comb-over, you haven't lost your post-baby weight since your last pregnancy—ten years ago, you have a lisp, your mother-in-law thinks you're a loser, your boss passed you over for a promotion again, or your sense of fashion favors dress-black socks with sandals. On the Internet, if you are quick with your typing fingers, you can click someone to an orgasm from the safety and security—and privacy—of your home.

Married and looking? Turn on your computer. WillyBoy is waiting!

8

THE WHITE HOUSE STAFF
or: A Guide to Presidential Pussy

Just a few years ago the media wallowed in the sexual exploits of Bill Clinton. Not only was the president brought to the brink of impeachment by Little Bill, his family suffered enormous and repeated humiliations as the minutiae of his proclivities became public domain. Fellow Americans learned Bill liked the tingle brought on by Altoid breath mints during a blow job, and that sometimes a cigar is more than just a cigar.

It was scandal at its finest. Public opinion divided over whether the Presidential Penis ought to come under some sort of penal code. Feelings about the whole ignominious mess ranged from apathy to outrage. In the end, two things became abundantly clear:

1. The nickname Tricky Dick was applied to the wrong president.

2. The days when the media carefully airbrushed mistresses out of the presidential picture were definitely over.

Because our chief executive is chosen by general election, you can assume that most of them have been somewhat charismatic to start with. (There are, of course, some exceptions, but isn't that what makes a rule?) Add to that power and fame—both potent aphrodisiacs—and you get the winningest pickup line in the Free World: "Would you like to come up and see my presidential seal?"

The thing that makes Clinton different is not the extent to which he took advantage of his appeal, but that his escapades came under scrutiny while he was still in office. As you will see in this chapter, many of his predecessors were guilty of dipping their wicks in all sorts of places, but most of them were protected rather than prosecuted.

So, from the documented to the alleged, here are some tales of the First Penises.

NOW, THAT'S A FASHION REVOLUTION

Before George Washington fathered the country (and owned up to it), the colonial folks had a series of English barons, lords, and other titled fellows as their fearless leaders. Quite a few of these guys, it seems, were sent to the New World by those who wanted to get them out of the Old World as quickly as possible. One such man was Edward Hyde, whose title was Lord Cornbury.

After Lord Cornbury was made New York's governor-general, he sailed over from England and immediately scandalized his colonial subjects by addressing the New York Assembly in drag. When asked why he was wearing women's clothing, he gave the rather lame explanation that he was honoring the Queen by representing her so accurately. Although they didn't buy this rationale, blasé New Yorkers, hoping he would tire of the charade, allowed Lord Cornbury to flounce about in hooped skirts, flowing gowns, and fancy headdresses for quite a few years. But things got worse instead of better and, to add insult to injury, Cornbury was terrible at his job.

And then he began demanding that those around him refer to him as "His High Mightiness."

He had his portrait painted in cross-dress. He stole most of his wife's clothing. He stopped even pretending to do his governor-general duties. When the long-suffering Lady Cornbury passed away, His High Mightiness went to the funeral in drag. The New York Assemblymen considered this the last straw and, really pissed, proceeded to remove Cornbury from office.

In Cornbury's defense, his antics and misbehaviors increased anti-British sentiment and fed the growing enthusiasm for revolution.

GEORGE DOESN'T EVEN PLUCK A CHERRY

It seems the father of our country never fathered anyone, he never cut down that famous cherry tree, he didn't much like his mama, and his bride, Martha, was no virgin when he married her. In fact, all the women in his life were married either before or during their relationships with him, so he probably never plucked any cherries at all.

Despite his rather dour countenance on the dollar bill, George was a bit of a hunk in his youth. He had a strong, athletic build: He was about 6 feet tall and was considered quite handsome. These assets didn't help him in the romance department, however, as George wasn't very lucky in love.

As a teen, he became infatuated with the next-door neighbor's wife, Sally Fairfax. He began a lifelong relationship with her, one that grew over the years and was certainly reciprocated. Whether he and Sally ever did the horizontal bop has remained a point of speculation for historians, but that Washington loved Sally deeply is not disputed. Mrs. Fairfax helped prepare the undereducated, unrefined Washington for higher society by teaching him everything from literature and math to table manners and the art of genteel conversation.

George, whose family had no money to speak of, proposed marriage to two different women and was turned down for lack of funds in both cases. Eventually he met and married Martha Custis, a plain, slightly older woman, who had been widowed and left with two children, but who came to the union with some much-needed cash. George might have married Martha, but it seems he still held a torch for Sally: He kept writing her love letters all through his engagement.

The false rumors that hounded George Washington were far spicier than his actual life. These included claims he was the real father of Alexander Hamilton, and that he had black slave mistresses (this was apparently Thomas Jefferson's department). Both rumors were well circulated at the time, but each appears unfounded.

BO-RING (OR GOOD AT KEEPING THINGS QUIET)

The most interesting thing about second president John Adams'
sex life is that he publicly proclaimed he was celibate prior to
his marriage with Abigail. Adams appears not to have dallied
outside his marriage, which is surprising given his frequent and
often lengthy absences from home. Once he spent an unbroken
nine-year stretch with an ocean between him and his wife!

His ability to keep his libido in check didn't mean his family
life was all smooth sailing, however. Adams and his son, John
Quincy (president number six), are two parts of a perfect pro-
totype for the quintessential dysfunctional political dynasties
that have made America great. John's two younger sons died
hopeless alcoholics, and John Quincy, well, we'll be discussing
him later.

JEFFERSON LOVES EVERYBODY

Thomas Jefferson, Lothario Extraordinaire, didn't seem to care
whether his women were married or otherwise off-limits. The
first of his many infamous affairs was with Mrs. Betsy Walker,
the wife of a friend, John Walker. Jefferson was so close to the
couple that he served as an usher at their wedding, but that
didn't stop him from pursuing Mrs. Walker relentlessly and
eventually seducing her, causing quite a ruckus. Some 30 years
later, Jeffie almost lost his life in a duel over what became
known as "The Walker Incident."

After Jefferson's wife, Martha, died, he traveled to Paris
where he met and became enamored of Maria Cosway. She
was an Italian artist and model married to another artist, Rich-

ard. A short, apelike man, Richard apparently liked women as models for his artwork, but as little more. Maria, a beautiful blue-eyed blonde, said she married Richard to avoid a life in the convent and to gain financial stability. All in all, your average lovely couple who sincerely despised one another.

Jefferson extended his stay in Paris because of his attraction to Maria and spent all his free time with her. When she and her simian husband went back to Italy, the future president was devastated. To soothe his broken heart he started carrying on with Angelica Church. Angela was not only married, she was a friend of Maria's. Needless to say, it created a bit of tension between gal pals.

(In America, his relationship with Abigail Adams, wife of John Adams, came under suspicion when T. J. sent her silk stockings from Paris and compared her to Venus.)

But Jefferson's most scandalous sexual liaison was with Sally Hemmings. Sally was a slave in Jeffie's house and, in a strange twist of fate, the mulatto half-sister of Jefferson's wife, Martha. (They shared the same father—John Wayles.) The affair between Sally and T. J. produced five children, one of whom was sold into prostitution in New Orleans—allegedly with her father's knowledge.

The Hemmings affair became public thanks to James T. Callender. Depending on your viewpoint, Callender was either a journalist or a muckraker. Earlier in his career, he had criticized John Adams so severely in an editorial that he was indicted under the Sedition Act. Even earlier, he'd earned his stripes by revealing Alexander Hamilton's extramarital romance, ruining, some speculate, the ambitious go-getter's chances of ever becoming president himself.

Anyway, Callender's anti-Adams campaign had helped Jefferson's career, and Jefferson considered Callender an ally. But once the political honeymoon was over, Callender turned his sights on his old friend and exposed his sexual activities with Sally.

Hysterical historians contested the accusations regarding Sally for decades. Impossible! Unthinkable! Dirty stinking lies dreamed up by the nefarious, evil Callender! As proof, they cited Jefferson's often expressed "aversion to the mixture of color in America." Jefferson, these historians claimed, could not have made such statements if he had fathered a brood with Hemmings. Why, that would have been hypocritical, and that would be unthinkable! Impossible!

Public opinion swayed back and forth on the issue until recently, when the descendants of Sally Hemmings underwent DNA tests. The test proved conclusively that Thomas Jefferson was their ancestor.

An interesting tidbit about Jefferson's administration: His second vice president was George Clinton. Unlike the Clinton inhabiting the White House in the 1990s, George didn't dishonor his administration with sexual antics. Instead this Clinton was remarkably senile and caused a different kind of problem with his inability to reason clearly.

M & M

James Madison was a tiny little guy who suffered from epilepsy. He was engaged to a woman named Kitty Floyd, who dumped him by sending a Dear John letter that she sealed with, of all things, a wad of rye-bread dough. Not exactly true love. But Madison rallied. He met and married Dolley Todd, a friendly, buxom woman, known as a warm and gracious hostess. Dolley Madison was the target of many vicious rumors, including accusations that she slept with Aaron Burr, Thomas Jefferson, and most of Congress. There isn't any indication that those rumors were true.

Elizabeth Monroe, Dolley Madison's successor as First Lady, couldn't have been more different. Highly unlikely to inspire salacious rumors, Mrs. Monroe was mostly known for her snobbery. Her husband evidently behaved himself, but his brother, Joseph, was a precursor to certain other embarrassing first brothers. . . . Joe was married three times and has been described as a ne'er-do-well lover boy.

THAT SON OF A PRESIDENT!

His brothers may have been duds, but John Quincy Adams faithfully followed in his father's footsteps, right into the Oval Office. His wife, Louisa, was a bit of a loony, scarfing down chocolate until her teeth literally rotted out of her head. She periodically spent weeks at various sanitariums and health spas. Once home, she would go on another chocolate binge. Meanwhile, her husband was repeatedly spotted swimming nude in the Potomac.

Skinny-dipping aside, John Quincy managed to keep his one-eyed snake out of trouble. That's not to say he could control the activities of his fellow politicians. House Speaker John Taylor was actually voted out because he kept his girlfriend in a Washington, D.C., apartment, where he was allegedly "sleeping with her every night"!

Adams and his wife had two sons, one of whom they named

George Washington Adams. George was slated to become the next in the presidential dynasty, but he preferred opium, alcohol, and women. He impregnated a maid and then committed suicide at the ripe old age of 27.

THAT'S BIG OF YOU. WAIT, NO. THAT'S BIGAMY!

Andrew Jackson was accused of adultery and his wife accused of bigamy long before he was elected president. The situation was, in fact, quite accidental. Rachel was a sweet and simple woman who, as a teenager, had been married off to Captain Lewis Robards. The captain proved a cruel and insanely jealous man and Jackson, a new attorney (and aspiring Prince Charming), heroically helped Rachel escape the evil Robards. He promptly fell in love with her himself.

As Rachel's lawyer he set the paperwork for a divorce in motion. When Robards eventually sent word that his marriage with Rachel had been annulled, Andrew and Rachel married, probably expecting to live happily ever after. But there was a bit of a problem. The duplicitous captain was lying. He didn't actually obtain an annulment and Rachel was—on paper if not in practice—married to both men for a couple of years.

The effect on Rachel's reputation was devastating. Jackson fought several duels in defense of her honor, but Washington society still never accepted her.

Sadly, Rachel died just weeks before Jackson's inauguration. Jackson went to the White House a cranky old man with an overblown sense of chivalry, which led to the dissolution of his entire cabinet over another woman's honor.

Although he was never personally involved with her, Jackson

felt the need to protect Peggy, wife of a friend, Senator John Eaton. Peggy came from common stock and had a colorful past. The Washington society ladies hated her, gossiping maliciously and snubbing the couple completely. Probably because of his experience with Rachel, Jackson felt compelled to force a fight over the issue. Instead of resolving it, he started a political storm, which ended with everyone choosing sides and most of the cabinet members leaving office.

The funny thing is, after John Eaton died, Peggy ended up in a real scandal. The middle-aged matron married a 20-year-old dance instructor. Shortly thereafter the dance instructor ran off with Peggy's own granddaughter and most of the family fortune!

YOWSA! IS THAT A JOHNSON YOU'VE GOT THERE?

The next resident of the big house was Martin Van Buren. Marty was a tiny, tubby guy described as a "dapper dresser" and a "preening peacock." All his fashion sense, however, didn't bring the women running. Or perhaps he wasn't all that interested. On the other hand, Richard Johnson, Van Buren's vice president, kept Washington tongues wagging.

Again, it's the black-slave-as-mistress story. Johnson fathered two daughters with a woman named Julia Chinn. When Julia passed away, Johnson brought the two mulatto girls to live with him in Washington. He took them to social functions and expected his contemporaries to overlook the girls' illegitimacy as well as their color—an unheard-of attitude at the time. Needless to say, it was a bit shocking for Washington society, not to mention its then-delicate sensibilities. Of course, it was no more scandalous than the fact that Johnson lived with a succession of lovers, some of whom were Native American, some of whom were black.

If Johnson had political aspirations of knocking the vice off his title, his personal johnson and its penchant for more exotic women certainly killed his chances.

Following Van Buren was William Henry Harrison, a.k.a. "Tippecanoe." Harrison didn't have much time to fool around in the Oval Office because he was too sick. Inept and bizarre medical procedures helped kill him; he was dead thirty days after his inauguration. He must have been gettin' some before he got sick though, because he fathered ten children.

Vice President John Tyler took Harrison's place. It appears that during his administration Tyler was too busy trying to fend off impeachment proceedings to bother sticking his willie where it oughtn't go.

A POLK WITH NO POKE

President Polk apparently led a life that was pretty pokeless. He married the daughter of a very wealthy merchant, Sarah, who came to the marriage with some serious opinions about the nature of frivolity: There was to be no fun of any kind in the White House. Sarah did not believe in dancing. She did not believe in theater. Her husband deferred to her on such matters.

In fact, the Polks were so uptight, that when the Whigs tried to damage Polk's reputation, they found him completely invulnerable to personal attacks. Instead, they tried to rake up some political scandal—without much luck. So the pokeless, danceless, boring Polks left the White House without the taint of scandal . . . unlike . . . well, we'll get into JFK later.

BARNYARD ANIMALS

Zachary Taylor, who followed Polk into office, didn't stir up any sexual controversy either. Besides, it wasn't women Taylor adored so much as his horse, "Old Whitey." Seems Taylor had quite a soft spot for his horse . . . or maybe it was soft *because of his horse.* He rode Old Whitey so much that he became bow-legged, he chewed tobacco, and he had terrible manners. But then again, compare Taylor's chewing tobacco with Clinton's cigars, and the old boy has little to worry about.

WHAT'S IN A NAME?

From Taylor to the Fillmores to the Pierces, scandal didn't rock the presidency much. With a name like Millard Fillmore, you think the guy's going to get lucky?

In the case of the Pierces, President Franklin was considered quite a looker, and women were invariably attracted to him. However, he came to the presidency with the aura of tragedy about him. Just prior to taking office, he, his wife, and his only son were riding in a train that crashed. His son was crushed to death. His wife became so depressed and grief-stricken that she remained cloistered from Washington society and walked almost bent over. For sad reasons, Pierce wasn't piercing much of anything during his presidency.

TAKE MY WIFE, PLEASE

Have we ever had a gay president? While most might answer "no," we actually have a strong candidate in James Buchanan.

Though as a young man, Buchanan had a tendency to form strong attachments to older men, including one of his professors at Dickinson College, he eventually became engaged to one Ann Coleman. She was the daughter of one of the wealthiest men in the United States at the time. However, in short order, she found Buchanan so cold that she determined he was after her money and she broke off the engagement. Shortly thereafter, she committed suicide.

When Buchanan was elected, the myth surrounding him was that he was so upset by the suicide of his former fiancée that he could not bear to enter another romantic relationship. Well . . . maybe not with a woman but . . .

Before his presidency (1857–1861), Buchanan had formed another strong attachment to a man, this time Senator William King. In fact, the two were so utterly inseparable—Buchanan once even wanted the senator to be his vice president—that both the press and the Washington gossip hounds took to calling King the president's "Better Half," "Miss Nancy," or, alternatively, "Aunt Fancy." And, on more than one occasion, Buchanan, Mr. Fancy himself, actually referred to Senator King as "my wife."

King died before hubby James became president, and Buchanan never went on to have any other romances. His niece served as his hostess. So were Buchanan and Senator King really getting it on? Historians are divided. At the very least, Buchanan and King had formed an attachment that bordered on romance.

SHE DRIVES ME CRAZY

Next we come to Honest Abe. As a young man, Abraham Lincoln courted a woman named Mary Owens. She was quoted as saying, after the breakup, however, that Lincoln was "deficient in those little links which make up the chain of a woman's happiness." So perhaps Abe wasn't too satisfying in a romantic way. Abraham Lincoln: tall man, deficient little link.

Abe eventually married another Mary: Mary Todd. This Mary was quite a handful. Insanely jealous, she would fly into rages if a more attractive woman was in the vicinity, often warning her husband "not to be flirtatious with silly women." Abe was often beside himself over how to handle his wife. He would sometimes have to escort her to her White House quarters after she made a scene. Though Mary seethed with rage over these imagined flirtations, it appears that Lincoln always remained quite devoted to her.

Eventually, the death of her son and personal sorrow drove Mary Todd Lincoln still further over the edge. Lincoln took to calling her "mother" to soothe her, and he referred to her as his "child-wife."

After Lincoln was shot, Mary Todd Lincoln's own sons eventually had her declared insane. They hired Pinkerton guards to tail her every move in an effort to keep her out of trouble, but this only made her more paranoid: Once she even hid in a rack of clothes in a store to escape the "evil men" pursuing her.

GIRLS DON'T WANNA HAVE FUN

The next three presidencies were occasionally tainted by scandal, but not the sexual sort. Andrew Johnson, Ulysses S. Grant (an alcoholic and all-around inept president), and Rutherford Hayes kept out of trouble. If not always, in Rutherford's case, out of Lucy Hayes. . . .

In Lucy Webb Hayes, the nation again had a First Lady with no sense of fun. She banned alcohol from the White House, and though Rutherford liked his occasional glass of wine, he deferred to Lucy's wishes, apparently not wanting to be "cut off" in the bedroom. Eight kids in twenty years . . . he was busy. Too busy to worry that the White House was becoming boring.

WHAT??? POLITICAL SCANDALS AND IRONY?

James Garfield ran for president while the country was reeling from one political scandal after another. Shady investments, wives taking kickbacks, and clear conflicts of interest had all been exposed in previous administrations, causing the public to lose faith in elected officials. Garfield had an honorable reputation and was therefore particularly appealing to voters who were sick of Washington shenanigans. But Garfield wasn't as saintly as his constituents might have hoped.

Actually, James G. seems to have suffered from quite a bit of depression. Despite his often-expressed doubts about matrimony, he married Lucretia Rudolph and then described his years with her as "a great mistake."

He took up with a mysterious woman known only as Mrs.

Calhoun, and then confessed his adultery to his wife. She forgave him his sins and even gave him her blessing when he decided to travel to New York to see Mrs. Calhoun again—this time to retrieve incriminating love letters he had written.

Later, Garfield went off on a religious retreat (something he did periodically) and, while supposedly seeking spirituality, he rekindled a relationship with an old flame from his college years named Rebecca Selleck.

Garfield might have proven the sauciest section of this chapter, but unfortunately he was assassinated less than a year after his election, making it impossible for him to fulfill his true adulterous potential.

Bad doctoring and bacteria (it wasn't the assassin's bullet that killed Garfield, it was his physician's poor hygiene) ushered Chester Arthur into the Oval Office. Chester was a regular party machine. A widower who loved stylish clothes and late nights, he was accused of keeping a mistress in a secret room in the White House. Arthur complained that being a victim of such vicious talk was worse than being assassinated. One doubts that Garfield would have agreed with Arthur's comparison, but his whining did squelch the gossip to some degree.

THE TRUTH . . . WHAT A CONCEPT!

Grover Cleveland did a remarkable thing during his presidential campaign: He told the truth. And he got elected anyway.

Stephen Grover Cleveland was a big fat guy who, in his early days, was sheriff of Erie County in New York State. He and his cronies formed a club called "The Jolly Reefers," the main purpose of which was apparently to throw parties where the booze would flow freely and the women would prove agreeable. It was during one of these shindigs that Big Steve (as he was known at the time) allegedly met Maria Halpin and began an affair with her.

When Maria turned up pregnant, Cleveland took financial responsibility for the child even though he was only one of several possible fathers. Because he was the only unmarried suitor, Cleveland agreed to take on the child—for everyone's sake. While he was running for president, the newspapers uncovered the story of his bastard son. Much to many people's surprise, Grover admitted the boy was probably his, and the public didn't hold it against him. (Cleveland was most likely the kid's father: the resemblance was reported as startling.)

Cleveland got married for the first time when he was 49 years old. Detractors were horrified by his choice of mate—Frances Folsom, the 20-year-old daughter of a close friend who had known him as "Uncle Cleve" throughout her life. She and Uncle Cleve had five children together.

ZZZZZZZZZ

The next four presidents either kept their sexual antics very quiet, or they weren't very interesting. Benjamin Harrison was a tiny fellow whose grandfather was the 30-day prez, William Henry Harrison.

Little Benj got married when he was only 19 years old. He was apparently devoted to his wife, Caroline, and although his service in the White House wasn't scandal-free, none of it was caused by a wandering weenie.

Next up was William McKinley, a devoted husband whose wife, Ida, was by all accounts the love of his life. Their two daughters had both died, causing Ida to become seriously depressed. Some of his enemies tried circulating rumors that McKinley beat the moping Ida and ran around with other women, but no one fell for it.

After McKinley was assassinated, Teddy Roosevelt became president. He was 43 when he assumed office, making him the youngest president to do so. Unlike Franklin D., Teddy kept his love log firmly zipped in his pants. He did give us the phrase "Walk softly and carry a big stick," but he wasn't talking about *that* kind of stick, and he turned out a dud in the erotic scandal department. Roosevelt was succeeded by Taft, another carnally boring—if morbidly obese—guy. But then came . . .

AMERICA GETS A WOODY

Woodrow Wilson's wife, Ellen, died after 27 years of marriage, and the public felt sorry for the poor presidential widower. But the public can be fickle, and when they thought he was wagging the old woody around, the people became incensed.

First, rumors circulated about an affair with Mrs. Mary Hubert. But it was Wilson's passionate pursuit of Edith Bolling Galt, a plump 42-year-old widow, that really annoyed people. Wilson was so taken with Galt that he sent White House researchers to the Library of Congress to find love poems he could send her. A mere nine months after his wife's death he asked Galt to marry him. Although she put him off for a few months, she did eventually accept his proposal. During their engagement the *Washington Post* ran a hilarious typo. It reported that President Woodrow Wilson spent the afternoon "entering his fiancee."

Wilson and Galt married while Wilson was still in the White House. Shortly after the wedding, he suffered a nasty stroke. Some historians claim that for the remainder of his term Edith was the acting president.

WARREN HAS A HARD-ON

Warren G. Harding had quite the stiffy when it came to the ladies. He was a dashingly handsome young man when he met his future wife, a divorcee named Florence, a.k.a. "Duchess." Florence's father hated Harding, publicly denounced him as a "fortune-hunting nigger," and threatened to kill him. Florence married Warren anyway, but soon discovered he wasn't exactly the monogamous type. He had an affair with one Carrie Phillips that lasted 15 years and caught up with him while he was president. Phillips, who threatened to go public, was given $20,000 to keep quiet. But Harding hadn't actually yet cooled it with Carrie when he became hopelessly infatuated with Nan Britton.

Nan asked Harding for an employment reference (sound familiar?), which somehow led to a hot and heavy affair between the old president and the young woman. The Secret Service guys helped Harding get his jollies (sound familiar?) by preventing Florence from entering the Oval Office and catching the couple in the act. Nan got pregnant and had a daughter by Warren, who didn't deny the child was his. In fact, he financially supported her and her mother.

Florence wasn't stupid—she was pissed off. So she hired a private eye, the inimitable Gaston Means, hoping to get some dirt with which to smear Nan Britton's name. All Means came back with were dozens of long, passionate love letters Warren had written to Nan. Needless to say, Flo was not a happy camper. Shortly thereafter, Mr. & (the sincerely irked) Mrs. Harding took a trip to the West Coast. During the trip, Warren mysteriously died. It seems as if he ate some bad crabmeat and fell ill. But it also seems he was on the mend when, after spending some private moments behind closed doors with Mrs. H., he suddenly took a turn for the worse. Although there was speculation that Florence did her horny hubby in, nothing was ever suggested officially.

ANOTHER COUPLA SNOOZERS

Calvin Coolidge and Herbert Hoover managed to keep their respective one-eyed snakes out of trouble, which is good because FDR would prove to be philanderer enough to make up for many a chaste public servant. The most interesting thing about either of them is that Calvin Coolidge's wife, Grace, once went out on a hike that ran an hour and a half longer than expected. When the press made a few tongue-in-cheek references to her disappearance, Calvin immediately removed Grace's bodyguard, James Haley, from First Lady duty.

A LYIN' S.O.B. (SO WHAT ELSE IS NEW IN POLITICS?)

Franklin Delano Roosevelt, a vision of confidence in hard times, of resilience in the face of foreign aggression, and of strength in a maelstrom of political upheaval, was far from a vision of faithfulness in bonds of matrimony.

It is rumored that after six difficult pregnancies, Roosevelt's wife, Eleanor, stopped sleeping with her husband, fearing that she'd become pregnant again. She was supposedly repressed and easily embarrassed by playfulness. In fact, she told a daughter sex was an "ordeal" that women had to bear. Perhaps FDR just didn't have all the right moves, but he was a cad through and through, as we will soon see.

FDR's first major affair took place right under Eleanor's nose. While Lucy Page Mercer was Eleanor's social secretary, she and the president pursued a long-standing affair. One day, quite by accident, Eleanor stumbled upon love letters FDR had foolishly kept (what's with these guys who can't seem to keep their extramarital affairs secret?). Eleanor was devastated: the pain bordered on physical. However, resilient and tough at her core, Eleanor gave FDR two choices: end the affair or divorce. Her meddling mother-in-law, anxious that her son's political career not be ruined, insisted the two stay married and threatened to disinherit FDR if they didn't. And Mercer, a guilt-stricken Catholic (but not so guilt-stricken as to have avoided an affair with her boss's husband in the first place!), would never marry a divorced man—besides, he would be coming with a lot of baggage . . . namely a few kids in tow.

The two broke it off, but Eleanor, extremely hurt, had two more conditions. One was that FDR and she would lead separate emotional lives from that point forward. The second was that he never contact or see Mercer again. Number one, Franklin followed. But, like a true politician, FDR did not keep promise number two for long.

After his next paramour—another White House secretary—died from a stroke in 1941, FDR set his sights on royalty. By this point, he was thought of as the "king" of the United States. He had tremendous power and the people loved him. So when Crown Princess Martha of Norway moved stateside while the Germans occupied her homeland, King Roosevelt took it upon himself to make the first conquest on the Norwegian Front. For over four years, Princess Martha resided in nearby Maryland. Beautiful and regal, she visited the White House for a week at a time, and FDR often rode to her home at night. Her husband rarely traveled to the United States, and Washington gossips often referred to this as FDR's "royal affair."

But FDR wasn't yet finished with Lucy Mercer (remember—Eleanor's secretary?). Miss Mercer had actually gone on to marry a wealthy man, but she was widowed shortly thereafter and it didn't take long for FDR to once again break his marital vows to Eleanor—and his promise not to contact Mercer. Soon, they had taken up where they left off. In fact, their affair was so open that whenever Eleanor traveled (which was often), her own daughter would invite Lucy to the White House for lunch. The affair carried on for years. Eleanor even found out that FDR invited Mercer to all of his inaugurations—which she got to watch from the privacy of a presidential limousine!

In fact, when FDR suffered his fatal stroke, it was Mercer by his side. Knowing the end was near, she left quietly in the night and made sure Eleanor was called so she could be there for FDR's dying breath. How gallant!

Eleanor's own sexual life was scrutinized because of her "Boston marriage" with a dear friend, Lorena Hick. From their correspondence, some historians conclude that Hick was indeed in love with Eleanor. However, it appears Eleanor was simply following the fashion of the day and forming a strong attachment to another woman, as was common. Hey, it wasn't as if she could form a strong attachment to that cheatin' husband of hers. Lorena and Eleanor were indeed devoted to each other and remained so for many, many years.

To Eleanor's credit, she eventually forgave her traitorous daughter. She also seemed to make peace with her husband's White House wanderings. She consented, after contemplation, to be buried next to him. And the two rest side by side for once and for all.

BELOVED BESS

Harry S. Truman again seemed to restore a sense of marital decency to the White House. Married to Bess, theirs seems to have been a solid marriage. But it wouldn't be long before the White House was again rocked by infidelity.

EISENHOWER WAS MY PENIS!

While Dwight D. Eisenhower was stationed in Europe, as commander of Allied forces, he had a chauffeur named Kay Summersby. Attractive, but not beautiful—some said boyish—Summersby, it is assumed, carried on a serious and long-term affair with the future president. Not only did Kay drive the married Dwight around, she became his unofficial "fourth" at bridge games and a member of his inner circle.

At one point, it is rumored, Dwight considered divorcing Mamie and marrying Summersby, but at that time, it would have meant scandal and a black mark on his military career. However, Summersby did follow him to Washington.

Despite all the rumors, Dwight constantly reassured Mamie that he loved only her. And Mamie believed him. Supposedly she told friends that if any extramarital nonsense had really been going on, she would have handed Dwight his nuts on a silver platter. Not in so many words, of course, but she wouldn't have stood for it.

We might have believed Dwight, had Kay Summersby not authored a tell-all book called *Eisenhower Was My Penis*. Actually, it was called *Eisenhower Was My Boss*. Despite teasing the press that the book would once and for all answer all their questions, it is mostly full of engaging, up-close stories of Eisenhower. However, there's plenty to read between the lines—most historians assume Dwight was the one doing all the driving . . . into Kay that is.

JACK OF ALL TRADES

And now we come to the biggest presidential pussy lover of them all. John F. Kennedy. JFK was rumored to have said that if he didn't get laid at least every three days, he would suffer from terrible headaches. Guess presidential pussy was just what the doctor ordered, because JFK got plenty of it.

Rumors of skinny-dipping in the White House pool and of women being sneaked into and out of the hallowed halls of our nation's presidential residence have surfaced through the years, along with rumors of a top-secret ex-wife (no longer given much credence). While every rumor cannot be substantiated, a few are definitely worth mentioning and are largely considered true.

Let's start with Judith Campbell Exner. This attractive brunette told her story in a book entitled *My Story*. As the late Kennedy was much revered (to this day the Kennedy family still holds some incomprehensible sway over much of the public) and Camelot was still a myth, the book was a sensation and Exner was often vilified.

According to Exner, Frank Sinatra, a sometime lover, introduced her to Kennedy. Ted Kennedy apparently also made a pass at her, but she rebuffed him in favor of the Presidential Penis. Among the secrets Exner revealed: JFK angered her by asking her to have a ménage à trois with him and another woman; and his increasingly bad back meant she always had to ride on top—this made her feel more and more like someone who was simply "servicing" the Presidential Penis rather than an equal receiver.

However, the most damaging story Exner had to tell was that, while she was screwing our president, she was also screwing mafia capo Sam Giancana. According to J. Edgar Hoover's secret tapes, from 1961 to 1962 there were 70 phone calls made between Exner and JFK, and though Exner denied it, Hoover claimed some of hers were made from Giancana's house. This made the whole affair a breach of security (not to mention those pesky marital vows with Jackie). Supposedly the affair ended under all this pressure and scrutiny.

But JFK's penis was not to be stopped. Two blondes from the White House secretarial pool regularly serviced the prez. Nicknamed Fiddle and Faddle by JFK (at least he didn't call them Mutt and Jeff), Jackie reportedly called them "the White House dogs" (though really, wasn't JFK the biggest dog of all?).

JFK also appeared to have bedded Marilyn Monroe, and we've all heard the conspiracy theories surrounding her death. However, it was not Monroe, but lesser-known starlet, Odile Rodin, who caused the most jealousy and pain to Jackie, according to insiders.

And there's another mistress, who, like Monroe, died under mysterious circumstances. This one even more so. Mary Pinchot Meyer was a Washington, D.C., socialite. Pretty and vivacious, she was also a friend of Jackie's. A double-crossing no-good friend, but that's insider Washington for you. In 1961, Mary and JFK first slept together, and after that, Mary kept a diary of her goings and comings around the White House. Many times, when Jackie was out of town, Mary stayed over at the White House. She even allegedly wrote in her diary that she and JFK smoked pot, so much pot in fact that he suggested they stop "in case the Russians did anything," and he had to make a decision.

Eventually, the affair waned a bit, and JFK was, of course, assassinated. But the Mary Pinchot Meyer story does not end there.

On October 13, 1964, Mary was shot twice in the chest as she was out walking. She wasn't robbed or sexually assaulted, there was no apparent motive for the shooting, and no weapon was ever recovered. Eventually the police rousted a laborer, whom they accused of the murder. However, Raymond Crump, Jr., was acquitted as nothing really tied him to the crime.

But the Meyer story still does not end. Mary Pinchot Meyer was related by marriage to Ben Bradley. She allegedly asked him to burn her diary in the event of her death. However, Bradley supposedly turned the diary over to the CIA, through a friend of his in the agency, and it is rumored that the diary was destroyed by the CIA, and, along with it, evidence of JFK's illegal and immoral activities. Well, some of them.

LADY, MOVE THOSE FAT FEET!

Next we move on to another chronic philanderer, Lyndon B. Johnson. This effusive and outgoing president had an eye for the ladies. Despite years of messing around on Lady Bird, she felt ". . . he only loved me." She also felt he loved the world— all people, men and women—and a person like that can't be expected to keep away from half of the world—namely, the feminine half. Whatever.

But LBJ was a difficult husband in other ways. Demanding of Lady Bird, he allegedly insisted she wear red and yellow, and that she avoid anything that made her look fat. That included full skirts and T-strap sandals, which, he supposedly insisted, made her feet look chubby. Yet despite this, she remained unfailingly loyal to her husband.

SO MANY CRIMES, SO LITTLE TIME

Tricky Dick seems to have kept his dick where it was supposed to be. But then again, with so many misdeeds, scandal, break-ins, tapes, and political tricks to attend to, where would Nixon have found the time to fool around?

THE QUIET YEARS

Gerald and Betty Ford still enjoy an enduring relationship. She has candidly discussed her breast cancer, alcoholism, marriage, and children with the press, and she consistently remains one of the most admired women in America. Gerald, clumsy though he may have been as president, seems to be a generally decent husband. What a nice change for the White House.

From Ford we move on to Jimmy Carter. Jimmy and his wife also remain completely devoted to each other and, by all accounts, enjoy a stable and loving marriage. The only sexual blip Jimmy managed to stir was a *Playboy* interview in which he admitted to lusting but never acting on it. This made headlines at the time, but given his knucklehead brother's propensity for acting stupid (Billy Beer, associations with Libyans), this was much ado about nothing.

The Reagans swept into the White House with Nancy's astrologer and designer fashions. Again, not a whiff of scandal of the sexual sort, though between his marriages to Jane Wyman and the former Nancy Davis, Reagan played the field in Hollywood. Bedtime for Bonzo!

When you're married to a woman who looks old enough to be your mother, you might be tempted to cheat. In fact, a rumor circulated that Bush had enjoyed an affair overseas earlier in his marriage. However, tough-talking "read my lips" Bush vehemently denied it and the rumor faded away.

So the White House enjoyed a sexual lull. But that brings us full circle to Clinton. And . . . well . . . things got pretty darn busy in that Oval Office again!

What a couple.

The Republicans went all out for the 2000 election when they put *Bush* (George W.) and *Dick* (Cheney) on the same ticket. One can only wonder about this blatant attempt to make the formerly staid political party appear sexy to the American public.

BIBLIOGRAPHY

Bartlett, John. *Bartlett's Familiar Quotations* (14th edition). Boston: Little, Brown and Co., 1968.

Bart, Peter. "Rating Game Gets Gamier." *Variety*. Oct. 13, 1997.

Bassett, Margaret. *Profiles and Portraits of American Presidents*. New York: David McKay & Co., 1976.

Boler, Paul F., Jr. *Not So! Popular Myths About America from Columbus to Clinton*. New York: Oxford University Press, 1995.

Brodie, Fawn M. *Thomas Jefferson: An Intimate History*. New York: W W Norton & Co., 1974.

Bullough, Vern and Bonnie Bullough. *Women and Prostitution: A Social History*. Buffalo, New York: Prometheus Books, 1987.

Byrne, Donn and Byrne, Lois A. *Exploring Human Sexuality*. New York: Thomas Y. Crowell Company, 1977.

Cuneff, Tom. "Cool Is Too Hot." *People Weekly*. Sept. 4, 1995.

Dabney, Virginius. *The Jefferson Scandals—A Rebuttal*. New York: Dodd, Mead & Co., 1981.

DeGrazia, Edward. *Censorship Landmarks.* New York: R. R. Bowker Co., 1969.

D'Emilio, John and Freedman, Estelle B. *Intimate Matters: A History of Sexuality in America.* New York: Harper & Row, 1988.

Economist, The. "Hold That Tune." Nov. 28, 1998.

Etc. *Entertainment Weekly.* June 5, 1998.

Ernst, P. and Loth, David. *American Sexual Behavior and the Kinsey Report.* New York: The Greystone Press, 1948.

Evans, Bergen. *Dictionary of Quotations.* New York: Delacorte Press, 1968.

Feinberg, Barbara Silberdick. *American Political Scandals Past and Present.* New York: Franklin Watts, 1992.

Flexner, James Thomas. *George Washington: The Forge of Experience (1732–1775).* Boston: Little, Brown & Co., 1965.

Foerstel, Herbert N. *Banned in the USA: A Reference Guide to Book Censorship in Schools and Public Libraries.* Westport, CT: Greenwood Press, 1994.

Gilfoyle, Timothy J. *City of Eros: New York City Prostitution, and the Commercialization of Sex 1790–1920.* New York: W. W. Norton & Company, 1992.

Gordinier, Jeff. "Attention Kmart Shoppers." *Entertainment Weekly.* April 8, 1994.

Grunberg, Andy. "Art Under Attack. Who Dare Say That It's No Good?" *The New York Times*, Nov. 25, 1990, Section 2, pg. 1.

http://www.eonline.com/Hot/Features/Porn/index.html, copyright 1998 E! Online, site visited 6/24/98.

Kohn, George C. *Encyclopedia of American Scandal. From Abscam to the Zenger Case.* New York: Facts on File, 1989.

Lawson, Don. *Famous Presidential Scandals*. Hillside, NJ: Enslow Publishers, 1990.

Love, Brenda. *The Encyclopedia of Unusual Sex Practices*. New York: Barricade Books, 1992.

Mapp, Alf J. *Thomas Jefferson: A Strange Case of Mistaken Identity*, MD: Madison Books, 1987.

Masters, William H.; Johnson, Virginia E.; Kolodny, Robert C. *Masters and Johnson on Sex and Human Loving*. Boston: Little, Brown and Co., 1985.

Marsh, Ellen Tanner. *A Doctor in the House*. New York: Silhouette, 1997.

McCauley, Barbara. *Woman Tamer*. New York: Silhouette, 1991.

Miller, Hope Ridings. *Scandals in the Highest Office: Facts & Fictions in the Private Lives of Our Presidents*. New York: Random House, 1973.

Mitchell, Jack. *Executive Privilege: Two Centuries of White House Scandals*. New York: Hippocrane Books, 1992.

Noble, William. *Bookbannings in America: Who Bans Books—and Why?* Middlebury, VT: Paul S. Eriksson, 1990.

Palmer, Diana. *Man of Ice*. New York: Silhouette, 1991.

Panati, Charles. *Panati's Browser's Book of Beginnings*. Boston: Houghton Mifflin Co., 1984.

Panati, Charles. *Panati's Extraordinary Origins of Everyday Things*. New York: Harper & Row, 1987.

Rafferty, Carrin. *Even Cowboys Get the Blues*. Ontario: Harlequin Books, 1994.

Roth, Pamela. *Too Many Weddings*. Ontario: Harlequin Books, 1989.

Random House Dictionary. New York: Random House, 1978.

Rolling Stone. "The ratings game: the politics of parental-advisory stickers (on sound recordings)." Jan. 22, 1998.

Ross, Shelley. *Fall from Grace: Sex Scandal and Corruption in American Politics from 1702 to the Present.* New York: Ballantine Books, 1988.

Schuler, Candace. *The Other Woman.* Ontario: Harlequin Books, 1993.

Schumach, Murray. *The Face on the Cutting Room Floor: The Story of Movie and Television Censorship.* New York: William Morrow and Company, 1964.

Scott, Suzanne. *One Hot Summer.* Ontario: Harlequin Books, 1997.

Stockwell, Anne. "TV's Holy Wars." *The Advocate*, Feb. 17, 1998.

Stuart, Anne. *Catspaw II.* Ontario: Harlequin Books, 1988.

Time. "Music: Against Smut." March 20, 1995.

Whitney, Diana. *Barefoot Bride.* New York: Silhouette, 1996.

Variety. "Racy Classics Lose Battle With Turner." Oct. 12.

INDEX

Flynn, Errol, 114
Folsom, Frances, 152
foot/shoe fetishism, 97–98
Ford, Betty, 163
Ford, Gerald, 163
fornication, 15, 27, 31, 66
"Frankie and Johnnie" (folk song), 52
Freud, Sigmund, 12, 81, 101
Frolic magazine, 38
fuck, as a word, 52, 66

Gabor, Zsa Zsa, 123, 124
Gabrielson, Guy, 82–83
Galt, Edith Bolling, 153–54
Garden of Eden, 4
Gardner, Ava, 124
Garfield, James, 150–51
Garfield, Lucretia Rudolph, 150
gas pedal girls, 98
Gay Liberation Front, 84
Gay Sunshine Press, 51
Geffen Records, 52
gender confusion, 79
gender reassignment, 85–86
Gent magazine, 38
Georgia, laws in, 15, 16
Gere, Richard, 122
Germany, 72
Giancana, Sam, 160
Ginsberg, Allen, 41, 84
girlie magazines, 38
good-time Charlottes, 14
Gore, Tipper, 52
gossip, 110–15, 151, 157
Gräfenberg, Dr. Ernst, 23
Grant, Cary, 125
Grant, Ulysses S., 150
Greece, ancient, 2–3
    homosexuality in, 80
    prostitution in, 60–61
Gregory IX, Pope, 77
Groening, Matt, 63
Grove Press, 42
*Guide to the Correction of Young
    Gentlemen, A* (magazine), 45
gynecology, 4

Hair (stage production), 48
Haley, Jack, Jr., 124
Haley, James, 155
Hall, Jerry, 123
Halpin, Maria, 152
Hamilton, Alexander, 139, 141
Hand, Judge Augustus, 42
Harding, Florence, 154–55
Harding, Warren G., 154–55
harems, 59, 104
Harlequin romances, 121
Harrison, Benjamin, 152
Harrison, Caroline, 152
Harrison, William Henry, 146, 152
Hawthorne, Nathaniel, 7
Hayes, Lucy Webb, 150
Hayes, Rutherford B., 150
Hays, Will, 44
Hays Code, 45–48
Hefner, Hugh, 40
Hemingway, Mariel, 49
Hemmings, Sally, 141, 142
Hercules (Greek mythological figure),
    80
hermaphrodites, 89–91
herpes, 19
hetaerae, 61
Hick, Lorena, 158
high schools, 12
Hilton, Nicky, Jr., 124
Hindu religion, 4, 74
hippies, 83–84
Hitler, Adolf, 120–22
Hollywood
    gossip about movie stars, 111–15
    movies, 12, 44–49
homophobia, 36, 82–83
homosexuality, 15, 117
    in ancient Greece, 2
    censorship and, 35
    considered mental disease, 11, 18
    discrimination and, 19–20
    in history, 80–85
    laws against, 16
    poetry and, 41
    prevalence of, 85